W9-AXH-878

Book Bridges
for ESL Students

Using Young Adult and Children's Literature to Teach ESL

Suzanne Reid

The Scarecrow Press, Inc.
Lanham, Maryland, and London
2002

SCARECROW PRESS, INC.

Published in the United States of America
by Scarecrow Press, Inc.
4720 Boston Way, Lanham, Maryland 20706
www.scarecrowpress.com

British Library Cataloguing-in-Publication Information Available

Library of Congress Cataloging-in-Publication Data

Reid, Suzanne Elizabeth.
   Book bridges for ESL students : using young adult and children's literature to teach
ESL / Suzanne Reid.
      p. cm.
   Includes bibliographical references and index.
   ISBN 0-8108-4213-0 (alk. paper)
      1. English language—Study and teaching—Foreign speakers. 2. Young adult
literature—Study and teaching. 3. Children's literature—Study and teaching. 4. Young
adults—Books and reading. 5. Children—Books and reading. I. Title.

PE1128.A2 R454 2002
428'.0071—dc21

                                                                         2001054168

∞™ The paper used in this publication meets the minimum requirements of American
National Standard for Information Sciences—Permanence of Paper for Printed Library
Materials, ANSI/NISO Z39.48-1992. Manufactured in the United States of America.

Contents

First Encounters

THIS CHAPTER IS WRITTEN as an emergency manual for a wide variety of situations. It provides advice I wished I could have found in my first experiences teaching ESL students. Instead of addressing the problems, I just talked louder and faster and smiled so hard that my face hurt at the end of the day; I wanted to prove my good intentions. Somehow, I thought the students would adjust to my routines if we both just tried hard enough. Results were spotty.

For the past six years, I have taught in two different situations. During the summer I direct and teach in an intensive English language institute in which the whole class speaks Portuguese as their first language. Otherwise I teach or supervise small group or individual tutoring sessions, and teach classes that contain one or two ESL students among the majority of native speakers. This book addresses both whole classroom experiences and individual tutoring or small group sessions. In many cases, the adjustments for each situation will be obvious. Three years ago, three students arrived in January for an intensive semester in English. Surprise! While struggling to accommodate these students with three different levels of language profiency and three different personalities along with my regular classes, I became convinced that, whatever the proficiencies of a new student (or students), literature written and published for children and young adults is a valuable tool. The wide variety of high-quality trade books provides a valuable resource for teaching both content and language skills. Literature for children offers the support of simple explanations, pictures, and familiar examples. Both fiction and nonfiction can provide the scaffolding on which

English learners can build both content knowledge (history, science, geography, etc.) and knowledge of the language used in schools to describe and explore these different subjects.

In this book, I begin with material that may be painfully obvious to most teachers. A review of basic principles lays down a practicable ground for ideas about teaching new learners of English, and the use of literature for young people that is easily available in most educational situations makes these ideas practical as well. Most of you will be teaching individual students within a whole class situation, or directing tutoring situations, while some of you will be teaching whole classes or small groups of new learners.

THE OBVIOUS FIRST STEPS

1. *Welcome your new students with gentle and warm sincerity.* Smile but allow some space for cultural differences and personal diffidence. It's tough to be new, especially for students who don't even know the language! It's even tougher if they feel that people in their new environment consider them a burden. Your new students may look frazzled, dazed, or even defiant. If you can act delighted despite their reaction or non-reaction, you will reap the benefits later.

☑ Speak slowly but not loudly. Enunciate each word without changing its normal sound. (When one new student asked the difference between "Atlant-ta" and "Atlanna," I knew I was over-emphasizing my consonants!)

☑ Use simple language but avoid broken English.

☑ Ask your students to help you pronounce their names correctly. Practice and accept correction gracefully. Students learning a new language need to feel expert at something!

☑ If your students' language is a Romance language (Spanish, Italian, Portuguese, French), use Latinate vocabulary ("depart" instead of "leave"; "cafeteria" instead of "dining room").

2. *Gather as much initial information as possible about your students' situation and language abilities.* If you can meet with the parents and if they or other close relatives speak some English, or a translator is available, ask about the student's habits of speech as well as the ability to read or write. What do they like to do with their friends? What would they like to learn? What are their goals? In the classroom, try to inquire about the students' interests, goals, and social habits. These questions can elicit much information about the students' literacy skills and experiences, and they encourage open-ended answers that help assessment. These questions also compliment the students by assuming that they do read and write, and they show a respect for literacy skills in languages other than English. A growing body of research shows that speech and literacy skills do transfer across languages. This means that what students know in their native languages will be much easier to learn in English than if they have to learn new information, concepts, or skills at the same time they are learning a new language.

You may also be able to ascertain what kind of support is available for your students outside of school from their families and living situations. Perhaps your student is a beginner who knows almost no English and has only elementary language skills. He or she may be part of the migrant population; perhaps the father knows enough English to work, but the mother has been more isolated at home and may depend on other members of the family for translation as they become more competent.

Or your student may have lived in the United States for several years and may seem like a fluent speaker but lacks writing and reading skills. Some students with outgoing personalities become competent at communicating by using body language and letting others finish their sentences. They are often enthusiastic about learning but may have less formal experience with English language skills than it may seem at first.

Listen carefully and kindly to any attempts at communication from the student and family. Any interest and courtesy you can show now will encourage cooperation later on.

3. *Use props, pictures, gestures, and examples—anything to assist communication. Encourage all of your students to pantomime, demonstrate, draw, point, and translate.* A picture dictionary in English is useful at this stage. Simplify the language you are using, but don't water down the material you are teaching. Enlist the talents of your more fluent students to make the relevant concepts and information accessible to the more "linguistically challenged" students. A strong imagination and a dramatic flair are useful here.

4. *Encourage your regular students to learn as much as they can of the new students' first languages. Suggest comparisons of grammar, vocabulary, and sentence structures.* Ask them to help label important items around the learning environment with phrases in both English and in your students' other languages. Use sentences and phrases rather than single words to raise everyone's consciousness about general language principles. These methods will be particularly helpful for beginning learners of English who need the most encouragement and initial help, as well as for native-language learners who struggle with grammatical definitions as taught in standard textbooks.

5. *First Priority: A Positive Social Adjustment for New Students. Assign only one or two "buddies" for the first few days to lead each new student around until the school routine is familiar.* Learning to use a language in an academic setting depends on developing enough confidence to make mistakes. Nobody uses language perfectly at first, but if your new students feel that the classroom is a safe place to practice, they will progress more quickly. Share the responsibility! If you demonstrate that ESL students are a fascinating new experience, your native students will imitate you and will vie to participate. Avoid overwhelming new students with different ways of speaking, new names to learn, and new faces. Gradually, you can add more "buddies" for specific

classes and tasks to widen the new students' circle of acquaintances.

THE BIG PICTURE

Most researchers of language acquisition estimate that competent students immersed in an English-speaking environment can learn basic interpersonal communication skills (BICS) in two or three years. It takes seven to nine years to achieve the cognitive/academic language proficiency (CALP) that is used in textbooks, lectures, and most educational films and demonstrations. Even native speakers of English have trouble mastering the kinds of language we use in standardized tests and texts. What are you going to do?

Patience! Patience! Patience! Remember that all we teachers can do is help our students to learn more than they already know, and to maintain a positive attitude toward school and themselves.

Most of us learn by practicing what we want to learn, whether it's learning to walk, talk, or read Shakespeare. Our early attempts are clumsy, but we finally get the general idea. At first, all we need is enough to get around. (The first time we see or hear Shakespeare, all we get is the basic story.) The more practice we get, the more we are able to refine our steps, our English, and our appreciation of Shakespeare's genius.

FIRST WEEKS: WATCH AND WAIT

The excitement of trying something the first time often carries new learners through the tremendous effort needed to coordinate the relevant aspects of our mind and body in new patterns. But continued learning is exhausting; so many new noises, so many new directions, so much confusion, and so many questions overwhelm us and make us want to escape. We become quiet, agreeing to anything that will let us retreat. Your new students may seem unable to sustain their focus during the first week, or they may indicate that they understand more than they do, just to end the conversation and divert attention away from themselves. Remember how many aspects of the situation may be new to them.

Try to use the same phrases each time you address new students to give directions. Help them maintain a steady routine until it becomes a habit. If possible, ask a volunteer to provide them with a simple written schedule for the first days, or even weeks. Include times, places, and names of people they will need to know, but keep it simple. Reading in an unfamiliar language takes extra time and energy. On the other hand, make sure that each day's schedule is complete so that beginners, and even intermediate-level students whose memories may be overtaxed with new stimuli, don't have to bear the burden of remembering details.

At first, I am always amazed at how little language brand-new students seem to know—and how they seem to be either totally bored—or frustrated and angry. If I am patient (though this is not my natural style!), managing them and their environment just enough to make sure they are gaining confidence, I find that in a few weeks, most students begin to bloom. They have internalized their new routines so that they can now spend energy on increasing their language skills.

INITIAL DIAGNOSIS

Your first assessment of your students will come from your observations of their adjustment during the first week or two. Any formal testing before this adjustment will be fairly useless unless the student is familiar with the type of testing used and is good at writing and speaking in a new environment in front of new people. Common sense indicates that formal standardized tests designed for native English speakers will not provide a completely accurate evaluation of intelligence, knowledge, or skills. Can you imagine having your intellectual ability and achievements defined by your performance on a test in a foreign language?

If possible, delay any testing of new students for a few weeks until they seem comfortable or at least familiar with their new environment. Many schools use commercial tests designed specifically to measure language proficiencies of individuals. Beginning with simple questions (e.g., "What is your name?") and instructions (e.g., "Point to the paper" "Write your name here"), the test giver ascertains whether or not the student can hear and comprehend basic English. If so, the tester will proceed with an interview of increasingly complex questions until the student's level of comprehension and ability to respond is surpassed. The tester may then voice a sound and ask the student to repeat verbally and point to the appropriate letters or pictures. Students are sometimes asked to describe a cartoon or even a series of cartoons arranged in a story sequence. A few commercial tests commonly used in schools and suitable for both young children and adults include the following:

Language Assessment Scales (LAS): DeAvila, E. A., and S. E. Duncan (Linguametrics Group, P.O. Box 454, Corte Madiera, CA 94925).

The tester rates the ability of the student to produce English sounds, discriminate between phonemes, and comprehend spoken English in an interview of graduating difficulty.

Idea Proficiency Test (IPT): Dalton et al. (Ballard & Tighe, Inc., 480 Atlas Street, Brea, CA 92621)

Available in English and Spanish, this measurement assesses students' comprehension and their ability to speak with appropriate vocabulary and syntax.

Speaking Proficiency English Assessment Kit (SPEAK): (Educational Testing Service, Box 6155, Princeton, NJ 08541-6155)

Individual assessment of oral proficiency for advanced secondary and college students, graduate teaching assistants, and teachers.

Many other good commercial tests help describe the language proficiency of students, but it is important to remember that any diagnosis will be affected by the student's ability to communicate under the stress of a new situation. The disadvantage of these tests is that they are expensive, they take time and effort from general instruction, and they provide only general results. Many experienced teachers of ESL students suggest using observation and portfolios for evaluation before subjecting students to commercial or standardized tests. School systems and states have different rules about exempting ESL students from school- or district-wide tests or about how to report their scores.

PORTFOLIOS FOR SECOND LANGUAGE LEARNERS

✍ WRITING: *Collect samples of the students' writing (or drawing), both the works done by free choice and those done in response to written and spoken questions.* The students' initial efforts may be minimal and repetitive until they gain confidence in their new language. At first, a beginner may only be able to copy a few words or sentences, but this is a good start. Students with intermediate-level proficiency may seem stilted if they stick to the sentence patterns and phrases they know are correct. Even more advanced students may avoid handing in finished written pieces; they know their writing may reveal the holes in their language knowledge. Some students are adept at procrastinating with utmost charm. Practice patience, but also encourage experimentation by introducing a variety of prompts, providing short lists of new words and phrases, and modeling various types of writing such as dialogues, letters, poems, and descriptions. Many books for young readers work as models for writing. Even basic-level students can copy simple text and subsequently substitute appropriate words as they learn them. Books written as diaries, letters, or collections of poetry provide similar models for more advanced learners. Suggestions for using books as models for writing follow in later chapters.

◀» PRONUNCIATION AND SPEAKING: *Ask an assistant or volunteer to tape the student reading aloud.* Select several passages ranging from the easiest possible to those which cause the student to stumble slightly. At first, basic-level students may only be able or willing to repeat simple phrases or numbers. Some students like to hear their voices played back, but this makes others shy. More advanced students with a higher level of confidence will most likely benefit most from this experience, as beginners often are too embarrassed to note anything but their errors.

Videotape several short conversations between new learners and others, both with students of their own age group and with adult teachers, to assess interaction skills. If possible, include a tape of a conversation with someone who speaks the student's native language to get a sense of the student's general language abilities as well as the student's abilities in English. Audiotapes will be adequate if the student speaks fluently without depending on gestures and body language to complete thoughts. These tapes will be useful in assessing cultural differences in communicating with peers and adults.

📖 READING: After new students seem to have recovered from the first shock of a new place, *ask them to read aloud a short paragraph from a book written for young people*. For students who seem to know very little language, first read the passage aloud, slowly and clearly, but with appropriate emphasis; you may even read the passage twice if the student seems shy or reluctant. If the student can repeat the passage fairly accurately with the appropriate rhythms, you may be able to ascertain whether he or she has the ability to decode English. Of course, this is only the beginning of reading for information, which necessitates comprehension, but it is a good start in assessing proficiency in pronunciation and sound discrimination. Comprehension can be assessed either by asking students to explain in their own language, or to place pictures representing the text in the proper sequence. After hearing an episode in a story, students can also predict what might happen next, either by giving a brief description or by drawing a likely scenario. Assessment of reading comprehension is difficult if the student does not speak a language understood by the tester, but it is not impossible.

Use individual books for children and young adults as a basis for teaching other language skills while providing information about history, science, geography, culture, and other school subjects. Trade books, that is, books published for recreational reading, are often more fun and attractive than textbooks, and they allow a huge spectrum of choice. The next chapters will explain the logic of this idea.

CHAPTER 2

Literature in the ESL Classroom:
A Rationale

WHEN WE PRACTICE LANGUAGE—or walking—we begin by approximating the finished product as much as possible. This process is different from mastering discrete parts of a skill in an orderly progression. The idea that learners should try to imitate the whole skill, even clumsily, before refining any of the component parts is a basic tenet of the whole language theory. Common sense would indicate that just being in a new environment where you must hear, see, and communicate in a different language would lead to learning. Rapid immersion does work, just as throwing someone into a swimming pool leads to swimming—sometimes. But when my husband once tried to use this method to teach our three-year-old daughter to swim, he inadvertently scared her so much that she avoided the edges of anything wet for a long time. Eventually she did learn to swim, but it took longer than it might have, and she never liked it as much as our younger son who was introduced more methodically and slowly. To be fair, some people seem to like risks and adventures more than others. My daughter likes to know what's happening ahead of time; she's more organized than my son, who files with piles on the floor and is, to be polite, spontaneous. However, my son learns new languages more readily and thoroughly than my daughter, though perhaps not as correctly. Personality does matter in language learning.

Anyone who knows more about whole language theory than the rough one-line definitions that cause so much argument realizes that simple immersion is not the most efficient way to learn a language. Hearing and seeing language as it is used normally, that is, in its "whole" form, is the first step. It *is* necessary to perceive the target in learning anything. Just as babies walk and even talk better if they crawl before they walk, new language learners succeed faster when they have a chance to listen first, to practice discriminating the specific sounds of English, the rhythms of regional dialects, and the peculiarities of individual accents.

The first step in teaching a language is to allow students time to hear and see the target language in a form that is comprehensible. This is a basic tenet of Stephen Krashen's Input Hypothesis (1982), which indicates that language is most efficiently learned by hearing and using phrases and sentences in a natural setting, leading to an acquisition of grammatical rules that seems instinctive. This is a good first step. How do you make that happen in a classroom? Whether you have one or more new learners, the following suggestions should help.

SEEING AND HEARING ENGLISH THROUGH READING

1. *Label objects in the classroom and other environments.* Label them in simple phrases or sentences that reflect commonly used sentence patterns. (Please open the door. Shut the door. This is the cafeteria where we eat lunch. Please sit down in the chair.) When you label, try to remember what phrases YOU use, and be conscious of the exact words you use. A few weeks after one of my students arrived, he asked me why I had asked him to "Take a chair"; where should he take it? Without thinking enough, I answered, "Oh it's just another way of saying, 'Have a seat.'" Immediately I realized how confusing I could sound. The labels should sound more like what students hear in the classroom, but they should also make sense to a new learner of English.

2. *Speak slowly and clearly.* Try to use simple phrases that you or others can demonstrate. Say as little as possible until new students absorb the environment and routines of the school. This is difficult

for me to remember; I tend to chatter, which can be more distracting than welcoming.

3. *Let new students participate as much as possible without worrying about what is being retained.* Beginners may be learning more silently than you know; the students are learning how to manage in a new environment. In a class of new language learners, the more recent participants are watching old hands to see what behaviors are acceptable to their peers as well as to the teacher. Classroom culture, as well as language, is being absorbed.

NEW INFORMATION

New information that is unstructured and new language that is not practiced regularly can be difficult to remember. People need repetition and structured input to retain what they take in. One way to ensure structured practice in listening—that is, interpreting what you are hearing into meaningful thoughts—is to repeat the same language exercises every day.

Before and during World War II, teachers using the Audio-Lingual Method (ALM) developed highly structured exercises of sentence and phrase patterns, which the student was to repeat faithfully. They were so boring to teach that language labs with audiotapes were developed to give the teachers a break. Unfortunately, students could parrot the phrases back correctly without knowing the meaning or even thinking. However, even this rote learning is useful in some situations when being understood is a practical necessity. Organized drills are convenient to help beginners learn handy phrases for daily living: "Good morning" . . . "Good evening" . . . "I need the bathroom" . . . "Hi. My name is _____. My address is _____. My parents can be reached at _____." Drills are also useful to help students internalize the building blocks for further skills. Such practice is useful in learning the alphabet and its phonic system, numbers and simple math facts. Simple poems, songs, and appropriate quotations can be used just to practice the sounds and rhythms of spoken English. New students of English need to get used to hearing their own voices speaking a new language. Humorous phrases and quotes can inspire a smile and a welcome from peers or other listeners.

However, memorizing formulaic phrases and sentences does not help students communicate in circumstances beyond a certain number of situations. In order to become a member of a community, new learners of English need to practice comprehending and producing natural conversation. They should to be able to "invent" their own phrases and sentences, relevant to their own experiences, needs, and wants. In reaction against the earlier use of highly standardized exercises and drills designed to train students to react with a practiced language appropriate for only a limited number of situations, language teachers now theorize that students need to practice natural conversation in social situations. Methods that emphasize dialogues, games, and relaxation make a communicative approach. Building on the precepts of whole language teaching, which emphasize the practice of fluency before correctness and precision are achieved in contrast to perfecting separate phrases and sentences, most current teachers encourage even new language learners to listen, read, speak, and write a wide variety of words, sentences, and even paragraphs before achieving perfection. Mistakes can be corrected after new learners have become comfortable participants in language communities. Paddling along in the flow of a new language, even with slow and clumsy strokes, is preferable and more productive than standing on the sidelines. Refinement of the details will happen once the rough motions are practiced and become automatic.

What seems most necessary for efficient language learning is an authentic purpose, a strong motivation to translate the sounds and symbols of language into meaning that the learner recognizes and can relate to former experiences. One convenient way to provide both authentic language and structured input is to use literature. Books and other written materials that have stories to stimulate memories of past experiences are authentic materials. They have not been written to teach a language (Collie and Slater, p. 3), but to enchant or amuse or interest any reader. In addition, a well-chosen literary work generally reflects cultural values while engaging the reader by addressing issues that are universally interesting. A good work of literature generally uses language carefully, compressing meaning, humor, and grace within a few pages, to make language that is worth the struggle to decode.

GENERAL PRINCIPLES IN SELECTING LITERATURE FOR TEACHING

1. *Allow choice if possible: people learn what interests them.* If you can allow a choice between even two texts, you are more likely to offer something within an individual's range of interest. Choice is also a psychological carrot. If I choose something, I am less likely to admit that I want to give up on it.

2. *Recommend works that are not too long or complex and that match the student's intellectual and maturity level.* Some students who are literate in their native languages will want to demonstrate their maturity by tackling literature that is on their mental level but beyond their linguistic level. Try to help them retain their pride by recommending well-known "classics" that are on their reading level.

Other students with a more basic level of proficiency in their native languages need books with short passages of text and many supporting illustrations. Provide trade books that are attractive, but not too difficult looking.

3. *Be aware of cultural preferences as well as individual differences.* Some situations that Americans define as humorous and light may seem silly or undignified to other cultures. Students and parents from other countries may expect a more serious atmosphere in a school, and may feel that they are being treated without due respect, especially if they are in a new environment.

4. *Avoid any stereotyping or phrasing that might be offensive.* Again, people in a new environment can feel particularly vulnerable and sensitive to possible insults, even when none are intended. I have seen students from South America stiffen when they hear the phrase "south of the border time" to denote a vague deadline, especially as some students are particularly careful to be prompt.

5. *Avoid dialect, jargon, or arcane subjects unless your student expresses a strong wish to learn these.* New students have most likely been exposed to standard English texts, and that is the dialect that will be most useful to them in academic and professional situations. Unless specialized language is immediately necessary for classwork, it may only confuse new learners of English. Unfortunately, many textbooks at the intermediate level and above are often particularly difficult for new language learners because they are written for various grade levels, and assume knowledge about the subject matter and its particular jargon that the new learner may not have. In order to include a wide range of subjects and material, textbooks often avoid repetition in language or illustrations. However, they do provide an organizational tool for learning a body of material. Introducing content material in trade books written for children and supported by good illustrations may allow intermediate-level students to use textbooks more effectively. Examples of different types of books are mentioned in succeeding chapters.

PROVIDING DIFFERENT EXPERIENCES WITH LITERATURE

1. *Encourage your students to listen to others read aloud.* Listening to literature is the basis for developing literacy in any language. Ask native-speaking students or students who are proficient in English to read slowly and clearly to new language learners, using appropriate expressions, sketches, role playing, and imagination to make the meaning clear. Reading aloud to someone with fewer language skills

is great practice for students who need to develop fluency and confidence. Use a variety of readers. Recruit volunteers.

2. *Use taped books.* This is a wonderful bridge for beginning readers and particularly helpful for non-native students who are also learning pronunciation. Commercial tapes are often available from public libraries or can be bought through a variety of educational sources. Tapes can be made by volunteer parents, college students, retirees, or anyone willing, but be aware that reading aloud on tape is not as easy as it sounds. Instruct readers to read the book first to capture the tone and avoid surprises. Read the title and author at the beginning of each side of the tape, and identify each new page number by whispering it so listeners can check their progress as they follow along. Number each side of the tape on the label. Don't forget to identify the edition of older books.

One expert teacher of reading, Connie Pravatt of North Carolina, suggests that struggling readers should first listen to the book at a slightly reduced speed. At the end of each chapter or section, check for comprehension with short oral reader conferences. After working through the whole book, readers can listen again at a faster speed to experience the book as a whole, and to practice a faster pace of reading.

3. *Encourage new learners to read as a way of learning to speak.* Reading literature obviously allows learners to review language in ways that speech can't. Words and phrases are frozen into place, for easy repetition. The visual cue of printed words is reassuring to a reader who isn't sure of where one spoken word stops in a phrase and another starts. Most current books that teach English as a second language (ESL) or as a foreign language (EFL) present the phrase "I'm gonna . . ." or "I'm gointa . . ." fairly early, because that's what most people hear when Americans talk about their immediate future intentions. Reading "I'm going to . . ." makes the grammatical sense of the phrase clearer and easier to remember.

Figuring out vocabulary from the context of well-written literature is more natural and valuable than wearing out a dictionary trying to decode a formal definition. A reader will quickly guess the general meaning of most words from the sense of the story, then refine or correct the more particular usage as the story progresses. Using a dictionary is difficult for many native speakers, much more so for new language learners. Computerized translators are fine for some emergencies, but often get in the way of reading or speaking. Picture dictionaries are helpful additions to any classroom.

SPEAKING AND WRITING ENGLISH THROUGH READING

The second step in learning a language is to practice speaking and writing. These are the expressive language skills, and are more difficult than the receptive or "input" skills of listening and reading. Again, literature for children and young adults provides a useful and enjoyable source for practicing these skills.

4. *Ask new learners of English to read literature aloud in a safe environment.* Reading aloud is a good start toward speaking, providing practice for the right muscles for English sounds to develop. Students get used to hearing their voices continue beyond single words and phrases. Let the student become familiar with the book or passage first, hearing it, reading it silently, and working out the meaning. Most important, avoid embarrassment! Tell listeners or coaches not to correct too many pronunciation errors at first, even if the sound drives them crazy. As much as humanly possible, make the first experiences of reading English aloud a relaxing opportunity for companionship. Enjoy the book together.

5. *Ask students to copy short passages from books they have heard and read.* For most people, writing for a teacher or even a peer is stressful, doubly so in a foreign language. Copying text is a nonthreatening way to begin. Obviously, this will be necessary practice

for students who arrive without any previous experience in writing or who have written in a different alphabet. In any case, copying sentences and short passages helps students absorb and internalize English grammatical structures. It also helps develop the eye-hand coordination so important in achieving correct spelling. The words used most frequently in English are often the most often misspelled, either because they sound similar to new learners of English (consider "of/off," "doesn't" as usually articulated—"dudn't" and "don't") or those pesky true homonyms which also confuse native speakers too/to; their/they're/there; no/know.

Copying short passages will take longer for new writers than for students who have many years of practice in hearing, saying, reading, and shaping the words. However, it is an important skill to practice daily, as it leads to more sophisticated writing. Students who have written in their native languages will often progress quickly after just a minimum of copying. Observing the new student copying a passage is one way to assess his or her familiarity with English. It will be quite apparent that some students may need no more practice in copying.

Literature written to be clear and accessible to young readers can serve as a useful scaffold, from understanding basic structures and vocabulary to practicing and eventually using a range of expressions, styles, and functions of language. The wide variety of subject matter, theme, tone, and language provides a great resource for new learners of English of all ages, proficiency levels, and cultural backgrounds. There are even picture books that use very simple language, yet are as sophisticated as any adult might want. Using such good literature can take the stress and drudgery out of the tremendous task of learning a new language.

CHAPTER 3

Multiple Passes

THIS COMPENDIUM OF IDEAS will help a teacher or tutor use a work of literature as a basis for lessons in listening comprehension, speaking practice, reading for themes and details, and writing more fluently and accurately. As students vary their focus with each reading of a work, they will deepen and broaden their comprehension. Most of us do not learn something the first time through. We recognize the big picture before we understand where the smaller pieces go and what they imply for the overall meaning.

Multiple passes through any written work will help students learn whatever language, information, and concepts the text may include. Children insist on that same song or book over and over and over again until they "get" it, often at the expense of the sanity of their parents—who wish they would "get over it!" As they become familiar with the shape, sound, sight, and rhythm of words, they can free their attention to focus on meaning. Once a person can comfortably translate those little squiggles on the page into mental images that relate to previous experiences or knowledge, he or she can focus on reading—making meaning from print. Once a reader grasps the general meaning, he or she can concentrate on the more complex or subtler issues of a text: the nature of the characters, the implications of the information, or the theme of a story.

Repetition is also soothing; it eases the struggles of absorbing so many aspects of a new language—its rhythm, its sounds, its structure, its grammar, and the quirky shortcuts that Americans use to circumvent grammatical rules. Some students will arrive in the United States more adept at reading than speaking because their system of schooling, in keeping with traditional pedagogy, has provided more practice in grammatical exercises and reading than in speaking and writing. Others are from cultures that do not encourage much oral communication in formal school settings, and this colors their use of English. Some students are just naturally quiet. Settling into a well-chosen book, either fiction or true, allows readers to practice those aspects of English which are least familiar to them; they are given a chance to become comfortable enough to take risks. These principles and strategies apply to ESL students both in a classroom setting and in individual tutoring sessions.

First impressions matter. Even when a student has helped to select a text, a good introduction can ease the ensuing relationship with the book. The authors of *Literature in the Language Classroom*, Collie and Slater, list several ideas for a successful "first encounter" (pp. 16–35). They suggest recommending a book that both you and your helpers really like. You should model genuine enthusiasm and eagerness, which is almost impossible to fake, in order to raise your student's confidence and curiosity. The following are some preliminary activities you could use when you introduce a book.

1. *Discuss the cover and the title.*

☑ Read aloud the title (clearly and slowly), and name any clues to the subject.

☑ Ask new readers to repeat the title, even in a rote fashion, emphasizing the correct pronunciation. Ask more advanced readers to name and describe what they see. Help them discuss the impact of the title and cover on a reader. If a student is a facile speaker but does not perform well academically, encourage him or her to practice comparing, contrasting, and describing aspects of the cover. Guide this type of student to notice various aspects of the book's format, such as the title and copyright page, directing attention to the difference between an author and an illustrator and explaining the significance of the date in an older book. Often these students need practice in focusing their attention on the significance of details.

2. *Capture and convey the mood of the book.*

☑ Use a guided fantasy, music, or facial and bodily gestures to establish the main tone of the book. This exercise should appeal to the intuitive side of communication, so don't worry about your reader's grasp of details. *For example:* You might play a tape of circus-type music for a happy-go-lucky story, or show photos of your family for a book about a home. Introduce a serious book with thoughtful words and quiet pictures. More advanced students might be enlisted to help plan this activity for other students.

☑ For nonfiction, the tone can be light-hearted, straightforwardly descriptive, somber, or even ominous. Try to communicate where the book's subject fits into the general scheme of your curriculum.

3. *Introduce key vocabulary and concepts.*

☑ Use pictures from the book and name the main objects, characters, and events.

☑ Draw, use photos, illustrations, or a picture dictionary to identify the main subjects. Ask simple questions about the subject.

4. Encourage beginning students to copy the title, author, and a simple sentence about the subject onto a page or folder that might serve as the beginning of a reading journal. Copying can help focus the reader's mind, and practicing the eye-hand coordination will make the particular shapes, letters, and words useful for writing about this subject. More advanced students might write a sentence or two to summarize previous knowledge about the topic or to predict how this book will treat the topic or what questions this book might answer.

Save further information about the author, the historical context, or other related subjects until after reading. Just get started!

START READING

1. *Read aloud first.* Read the first paragraph or page aloud, depending on the students' familiarity with the language and attention span.

Remember that listening to a new language takes a lot of mental energy, so avoid reading too much at once. Read clearly and fairly slowly but don't distort the natural sound and rhythm of the sentences. Try to relax your voice to avoid strain; focus on the meaning and tone of the text. This is harder than it sounds. Read ahead and practice the first pages.

2. *Shadow read.* Ask the students to read aloud with you as you read the text again. Read slowly, but normally. This helps new learners practice pronunciation and phrasing. Students with at least an intermediate level of proficiency will be able to read along more smoothly and faster. Even advanced students benefit from this step as they practice correct pronunciation. Many advanced students also need this step to practice reading fluently enough to pull the themes and general ideas of the text from the context. The temptation to stop at each unfamiliar word to figure out the precise definition is strong in many students of a foreign language. Shadow reading pushes advanced readers beyond this word-by-word stage into clustering meanings in larger chunks and, finally, abstracting from paragraph- or page-length passages.

3. *Ask the student to repeat each sentence after you read.* At this point, don't worry about whether or not your student is pronouncing each word correctly or understanding the whole picture yet. With more than one student, take turns. Keep the pace steady and use natural expression. If students ask about the meaning of a word or phrase, provide a brief explanation or translation, but try to keep the momentum going through at least a paragraph.

4. *Ask simple questions about the literal meaning of the main words and developments.* Don't explain in too much detail. Focus on helping your readers get the gist or the general idea of the book. The details will get filled in later.

5. Reread the first paragraph aloud, and then continue to the next. Let students hear where they have been, and then move forward. You may sense some consternation from students who are anxious about not understanding completely, but press on.

6. Repeat this pattern for a few pages or paragraphs, or until your readers look dazed. Pause for a quick review of the first section, and then give readers a time to rest or to react with spontaneous questions. If you can translate any of the text into a language more familiar to your students, do so. This clarification will allay their anxieties. If you are working with a group of new learners, let some of the more advanced or confident students explain what they have understood to anyone who seems confused.

7. If the pace is slower than expected, or finishing the book will take more than one session, provide a simple outline of the whole book (or of the next few chapters) after approaching the first section as described above. This nutshell abstract of the whole will provide a path for more detailed work, which some readers may need for reassurance. Making a simple outline for less capable readers would be a good task for students who may need practice in presenting material in an organized fashion.

FOR RELUCTANT OR BASIC-LEVEL LANGUAGE LEARNERS

1. Ask how to say something in the students' native language. Try to repeat it and accept correction gracefully. It will help your students' motivation immensely if they can laugh at you, but rarely should you express your own amusement at their errors!

2. If possible, try to find a translation in each student's own language. Let your student become the teacher and teach you in the same manner you are using. One student's embarrassment about his pronunciation was transformed into hearty laughter when I tried to read the first page of Jon Scieszka's *The True Story of the Three Little Pigs* in Portuguese, and his tensions eased permanently as we continued reading alternately a page in English and a page in Portuguese.

3. *Change books.* Help the student select another work if you sense reluctance. Perhaps he or she may feel too challenged, or, on the contrary, your student may feel insulted by the apparent simplicity of the book. Of course, you will not allow the student to switch more than once or twice.

SECOND READING

1. *After finishing the book for the first time, read aloud the whole book without interruption, letting students follow along looking at the text.* For a change of pace, allow advanced readers to read a paragraph or so and stop periodically to clear up any general questions. Encourage the students not to worry about details; the purpose of this pass is to grasp the general structure of the content and the normal flow and rhythm of English. An audiotape of the book or even a video of a longer work may be useful at this stage.

2. *For long or complex texts, provide a wall chart or time line of the book's structure to help struggling readers keep track of events and characters.* This can begin as a general outline that can be filled in with the relevant details as students grasp them. Don't spoil the ending of stories that depend on surprise or suspense, but lead beginning readers to the point where they might be able to make logical predictions. Good teachers will be able to judge how much guidance to provide.

CHECKING FOR GENERAL COMPREHENSION

The purpose of these suggested exercises is more instructional than diagnostic. Whether you are working with a group of new learners of English or a group that contains young or inarticulate native speakers, sharing the answers will help readers make sense of the story and encourage them to practice various levels of communication. Obviously, not all these activities will be suitable for all books or students. Avoid overloading students with activities that may exhaust their energies or interest in a particular topic or book. Maintaining the self-confidence of each reader should be a top priority at this point for continued learning.

1. *Together, help readers write a few sentences, each summarizing a section of the book or a part of the plot.* Each reader should copy each sentence on a separate piece of paper. Scramble the sentences, and then ask individual readers to rearrange the sentences in an appropriate sequence.

2. *Use the same or additional sentences to form cause-and-effect chains.* This kind of logic is essential to understanding academic and professional English, as well as much social communication, so it is worth the effort to ensure that students can use these concepts.

3. *Together, sort events and characters of fiction as "good" or "bad," "kind" or "unkind," "successful" or "unsuccessful"; or select other relevant comparison and contrast categories.* These concepts, like "cause and effect" in the previous exercise, may vary in different cultures. If international students are willing and able to explain any differences in the culture they come from, you can foster one more step toward global understanding. An easy way to illustrate categories is to use Venn charts for two or three characters or events.

4. *Together, list appropriate adjectives or adverbs to describe events or characters.* Keep this list available to students as a pool of new vocabulary for writing exercises. Students can also collect apt similes, metaphoric phrases, or other comparisons; they can post

them or keep them in a notebook for further reference. Again, students from other cultures may be able to share common similes and metaphors from other languages.

5. *Together, construct a simple graphic diagram of the plot.* As readers absorb more details, they can add to the diagram. With such a chart, beginning readers may be able to illustrate that they comprehend more of the story or subject matter than they can express in speaking or in writing. This plot diagram is useful as a basis for writing exercises, with a teacher or more advanced student providing the appropriate vocabulary and sentence patterns for new learners to copy.

READING FOR DETAILS

1. *Write a short series of questions about the book to check both literal and symbolic comprehension.* Begin with fill-in-the-blank questions to ensure that readers have followed the plot and have understood the relationship of the main characters. Next, ask short answer questions about how the theme of the story (or viewpoint toward the content material) relates to their own experiences. The purpose of these questions is not only to check comprehension but also to elicit discussion, to encourage students to practice related vocabulary, and to help them practice authentic communication — that is by relaying their thoughts to a listener. Ask readers to share their answers with a partner, then with a larger group. Follow up any initial conversation by encouraging comparison and contrast, clarification, explanation, and elaboration to practice academic language skills.

2. *Expand descriptive vocabulary by role-playing and demonstrating choices.* Ask students to think of a character from a book, then to imagine what that individual would be like in real life. Then ask some of following questions, providing a list of suitable choices for students to choose from in preparation for describing their character to the oth-

ers. Role-play or point to people in the classroom, photographs, or magazine illustrations to show the meaning of the vocabulary.

💡 What kind of hair does this person have? (Blonde? Straight? Curly? Kinky? Messy? Neat? None? Bald!)

💡 How does he or she walk? (Stride? Waddle? Shuffle? Glide? Slink? Pace? Stamp? Limp? Slither? Hustle?)

💡 How does he or she talk? (Chatter? Whisper? Whine? Gossip? Chatter? Lecture? Squeak? Scold? State? Define? Declare? Demand?)

💡 What kind of music does he or she like? (Rock? Classical? Elevator? Folk? Country? Jazz? Latino? Crossover?)

💡 What does he or she do for fun? (Sports? Roller-blading? Movies? Gossip?)

💡 What kind of clothes would this person wear? (Formal? Sloppy?)

💡 What is this person's favorite expression or phrase? ("You know what I mean?" "What's up?" "You listening?")

💡 What annoying habit does this person have? (Finger-tapping? Gossiping?)

💡 What is this person's major strength or virtue? (Intelligence? Generosity? Pride? Courage? Humor?)

💡 What is this person's favorite food? (Pizza? French fries? Salad? Chocolate?)

And finally: 💡 What is this person's name?

Provide adjective and adverb forms for nouns and verbs when it seems appropriate. Watching me role-play these various qualities (waddling and shuffling, whining and groaning) always brings a laugh to the classroom, while clarifying the connotations of many similar words. This is more difficult to do with a straight face in an individualized situation.

3. *Help students write biopoems about the book's characters.* I have used the following format for many years to explore my own impressions about myself, friends and acquaintances, and famous or

historical characters. I cannot find the original source, but I am grateful for this ingenious pattern. This works best when new language learners first cooperate to fill in the blanks to describe a character they have read about. Provide lists of relevant vocabulary for each line. I have provided an example from American history.

Line 1: First name:	*John*
Line 2: Four descriptive adjectives:	*Energetic, bold, active, ambitious*
Line 3: Relative of	*Father to John and Caroline*
Line 4: Lover of (3 things or people)	*Adventure, fame, and Jacqueline*
Line 5: Who feels (3 items)	*Pain, love, and power*
Line 6: Who needs (3 items)	*To win, to sail, and to strive*
Line 7: Who fears (3 items)	*Invasion, shame, and death*
Line 8: Who gives (3 items)	*Courage, pride, and energy*
Line 9: Who would like to see (3 items)	*The USA strong, united, free*
Line 10: Resident of	*Hyannisport and Washington, D.C.*
Line 11: Last name:	*Kennedy*

For newer learners, use fewer lines (or items) and work together as a group with a limited list of vocabulary.

4. *Use passages from a book to point out grammatical features.* For example, ask students to locate the words and phrases that indicate position in place or time. Or compare nouns preceded by "the" and "a." Ask more advanced students to rewrite passages in a different tense; or have them substitute singular subjects with plurals, and then make concomitant verb changes. Text with continuous meaning is more authentic than the connected sentences often used as examples in grammar books. Storybooks often contain extended examples of dialogue that use a wide variety of punctuation marks, in a more natural context than is possible in grammar exercise books.

INDEPENDENT READING

1. *Provide a few comprehension questions at periodic intervals of the text.* These should be designed to focus the reader's attention toward understanding the theme or overall gist. For beginning students, use a simple, routine format to build confidence: "What has happened so far? Who are the main characters? Which characters will probably succeed?" For intermediate students, vary the style of questions to expand their repertoire of academic strategies. "What are the problems being set up? What cause-and-effect relationships do you see?"

2. *Use simple crossword puzzles based on a text to provide extra exposure to new vocabulary.* Use synonyms and definitions for intermediate-level readers; for beginners, use sketches and add page numbers to clues. These help focus attention on the spelling and connotations of new words and phrases.

3. *Ask students to select and copy a few memorable quotes, and display them in sequence.* Students can then compare their selections and explain the reasons for their choices.

4. *Provide appropriate worksheets for at-home reading.* Ask half of the students to prepare the even-numbered exercises, and the other half to prepare the odd-numbered exercises. During class, pair students so that each partner has new material to share and explain to the other. The need to clarify their work to partners provides an authentic motivation for students.

5. *Invite interested students to prepare a montage of quotations from a book and illustrations, patterns, or photos from magazines to represent a personal interpretation.* This exercise can be highly attractive and motivational for beginners whose perceptions exceed their language skills, and for more advanced learners, it can

provide a basis for analytical discussion and writing as they explain their creations.

6. *Encourage students to read each other's work. Teach them to critique gently.* In a classroom where students can be trusted to work cooperatively (and that is not every classroom), ask students to trade their writing. Teach them to note two strengths of the work for every suggestion for improvement. Many students are motivated to write more carefully and tackle more interesting subjects if they know that their work will be read by their peers. This also provides models of good work for new learners of English, and helps native students to understand the difficulties of learning a new language.

ELABORATION AND ANALYSIS

1. *Listen to a recorded discussion about the text.* Record two or three native speakers talking either about their reading experience, their general opinions about the book, or their insights into the book's subject and themes. For basic readers, keep the discussion short and focused.

2. *Help students write a prequel or a sequel.* Lead them to imagine what logically could have happened before or what might happen afterward. This creative venture can be a good grammatical exercise as well.

3. *Help students describe what happens at certain points in a story, imagining that they are there but invisible, like a fly on the wall.* This exercise provides an opportunity to practice giving spatial directions as well as reinterpreting the story from a different point of view.

4. *Help intermediate and advanced students plan and make "Reader Support Kits" or "Book Boxes" for other readers to use.* Instruct students to select a book that appeals to them so much that

they want to know it well. Ask them to design three teaching activities that will

☑ Introduce the text by providing background information or new vocabulary;

☑ Guide readers though difficult passages with thought-provoking questions;

☑ Help readers summarize the content or story and think about issues raised by the text.

Originally designed by Robert Small, this exercise encourages students to become deeply involved in a book and to practice critical thinking as they design lessons for other students. They practice planning, writing directions, and gathering materials for appropriate activities for others. After they finish writing their instructions, they should ask another student to test them out, evaluating them for clarity and completeness. Make the necessary adjustments and improvements. To complete the Book Kit, decorate and title a box or folder with pictures and symbols appropriate to the mood, subject, and theme of the text. Include all the materials necessary to carry out the planned activities. Share kits with other students. Students who complete this project often become passionate about the book they have chosen; they come to know the book deeply.

In my experience, learning a language or any new information seems to be an interplay between sensing the general meaning of a subject or story; analytically exploring the themes, character relations, and plot developments; and finally comprehending the deep implications of all the details as we fix them in memory. Multiple passes through a book allow for this rich learning experience to happen.

CHAPTER 4

Using Picture Books
for Basic-Level Learners

BOOKS IN WHICH THE TEXT is supported by pictures and other images can be used to facilitate learning for students of all levels and ages, but they are particularly valuable in reducing the affective blocking or nervous tension that plagues so many beginners. This chapter will explain how to use picture books for speaking and writing prompts; for practice drills in pronunciation, grammatical phrasing, and composition; and for supporting more complicated reading.

Good pictures are as close to universal language as the world is likely to get within the next twenty years, and picture books are an invaluable aid to communication across linguistic lines. In the last few decades of the twentieth century, the variety, range, and sophistication of available picture books has increased astronomically. Before the middle of the twentieth century, book illustration was considered inferior to other fine arts; since then, both the status and technical quality of illustrations has improved immensely. Books for children are illustrated with photos, paintings, drawings, cartoons, and montage. They are romantic, realistic, or ridiculous—lush, bold, or subtle. All styles seem acceptable; experimentation is the trend.

It is important to be sensitive to students' personal and cultural preferences in selecting appropriate picture books. In some cultures, fantasy is considered silly and demeaning to all but the youngest children. For others, pictures or subjects Americans consider harmless or funny may seem gross or disgusting. The safest approach is to provide a variety and allow some choice, although most students will soon learn to adapt to the variety available from American publishers. Some new learners don't feel that they are progressing unless they are plowing through the type of grammar workbook traditionally used for language learning; others will immediately appreciate the escape from learning about the language and enjoy using language in a more contextualized and natural form. If a book doesn't "work," move on. Even discussing why a book is "no good" provides practice in language.

PICTURE DICTIONARIES

The most effective aid to communicating with people with limited English during those first encounters is a good picture dictionary, which matches pictures with common English words. Readers of other languages who are new to English appreciate the precise correspondence between the item pictured and its label. It's reassuring to find something definitive among the complexities of sounds and printed symbols. Although picture dictionaries are limited to naming things and actions, these names act as important stepping-stones to more complex communication. They identify needs and desires. They anchor events and situations.

Several picture dictionaries match vocabulary from other languages with English labels. These may be useful in bilingual teaching when reading and writing in both languages is the goal. For teaching fluency, however, the mental path between the image and the English name should be uninterrupted. For most learners, the goal is not translation; it is immediate association between the object or action and an English word or phrase. For beginning learners of a language who are beyond the age of ten or so, skipping the mental process of translating is almost impossible, so many new learners will prefer the extra clues of a dictionary. Try to help students avoid using dictionaries and mechanical translators as a crutch except when they are feeling intensely frustrated. Generally, after the very basic level, students should try to use context clues to find meaning.

One of the most popular picture dictionaries for beginners and intermediate students to expand their vocabularies is *The Oxford Pic-*

ture Dictionary compiled by Norma Shapiro and Jayne Adelson-Goldstein. The *Scholastic Visual Dictionary* is a new entry into the field, more suitable for older readers, providing more detailed labels about heavy machinery, biology, football, and other subjects related to more advanced learning. Both are inexpensive and easy-to-use, formatted like workbooks and arranged in a logical sequence for students or workers. A good picture dictionary for Spanish-speaking students is the bilingual text *1,000 Palabras en inglés*. The humorous illustrations are cute but not silly or childish, and the English and Spanish underneath are accompanied by the appropriate articles and, in many cases, prepositions. For example, nursery rhyme characters are placed in a scene labeled "in the enchanted forest." Other useful words include the ordinals, days of the week, and verb tenses. Less useful are picture dictionaries and encyclopedias that merely list the images and labels alphabetically, not presenting them in a life-related context in which the words would generally appear. Several encyclopedias published for young people have gorgeous illustrations, but are often so complex and ornate that they are difficult for new language learners to comprehend.

SPEAKING AND WRITING EXERCISES

1. *Practice Sentence Patterns:* For beginners and intermediate learners, drills in sentence patterns help develop habits of grammatical correctness and fluency. For ESL groups or individuals, use the picture dictionary to vary a noun or a verb, and to introduce new vocabulary.

> 📝 *Example*:
> a. The _____ likes to eat _____. (people, animals, food)
> b. May I have a/the _____? I would like to _____. (noun, verb)
> c. Place the _____ on the _____ over the _____. (nouns)

Vary the complexity of the sentences according to the language level. Ask students to write the whole sentence, filling in the blank with a different appropriate choice each time, so the pattern is internalized. Use the written sentences for drills in speaking correctly.

2. *Expand vocabulary by using the dictionary for categorizing games.*

> 📖 *Example*:
>   a. Things in the classroom.
>   b. Things I could carry.
>   c. Things I can do.

3. *Challenge more advanced writers to compose a paragraph to share, using five items from a selected page or section.* Writing exercises with clear limits are easier for most people and can be directed for practice of specific vocabulary.

> 📖 *Example*:
>   a. Something has been hidden in the classroom. What is it? Who hid it? Give directions for finding it.
>   b. Write about a visit to the grocery store (or doctor's office, etc.).
>   c. Describe two hours in the life of a _____ (doctor, teacher, baby).

4. *Keep picture dictionaries handy when reading or introducing books about new subjects.* These are a useful crutch for new learners, providing security as well as extra support.

PICTURE BOOKS FOR YOUNG CHILDREN

Since most picture books are designed for preschool and elementary age children, selection and use of these books with those ages will be relatively easy. Reading slowly and clearly, sharing delight in the pictures, and pointing out details come naturally to most educators reading to younger children. The only difference in sharing picture books with children whose dominant language is not English will be the pace of teaching and extent of their responses. Instruct volunteer readers to focus on making the experience pleasant and easy. Keep the pace of reading slow enough for a listener to absorb the meaning of the illustrations but fast enough not to bore the listener. If your student seems to lose interest before the end of the book, take a brief break before returning to the story. Let the child look at pictures without listening to the words, or even wander around for a bit. People listening to a foreign language need to rest their minds periodically. Remember that paying attention to a foreign language is more tiring than hearing familiar words and sounds, even with pictures. The goal is to provide opportunities for students to practice English: Push them gently to speak, read, copy, write, ask, respond, answer, compare, contrast, and even complain.

A FEW SUITABLE SELECTIONS

Molly Bang's *Ten, Nine, Eight* is a colorful way to review counting. It's simple, quick, and fun. A good book for elementary beginners is *Bread, Bread, Bread* with text by Ann Morris and photographs by Ken Hegman. This colorful review of fourteen kinds of bread from as many different cultures contains only about fifty words on twenty-eight pages with reassuringly large print. The vocabulary includes the names of some bread-related objects, prepositions, and verbs such as "making," "shaping," and "baking." These and the invitation to "Have a bite" comprise a useful lesson for interpersonal communication.

David Shannon's *No, David!* contains only three words, but the cartoon pictures tell the whole story of a boy who just can't get anything right! This book is a good way to break the ice in a class or in a tutoring situation, or it can provide a break at the end of a discouraging lesson. Encourage readers to use loud, expressive voices, but understand that for some, these outbursts may seem awkward or rude.

Margaret Wise Brown's quiet classic, *Goodnight Moon,* has little text, but each word or phrase is supported by the beautiful, satisfying illustrations. Most beginning readers of English, even young readers, could finish this book in a twenty-minute session. *The Runaway Bunny* by the same author and illustrator contains seventeen pages of text, also well supported by the illustrations. An attractive feature for beginning readers is the if/then sentence pattern, which is repeated throughout the book . . . until the end when the mother rabbit matter-of-factly advises, "Have a carrot." This is also appropriate for older readers who will appreciate the gentle tongue-in-cheek attitude of Mother Rabbit toward her young son.

SOME ACTIVITIES FOR YOUNG CHILDREN

1. *Read using the exercises suggested in chapter 3.* Picture books provide enough clues to the brief text that readers can absorb the language quickly.

2. *Repeat picture books regularly, even daily if possible.* Familiarity will reassure new readers. When readers indicate boredom, move on to other books.

3. *Ask leading questions to encourage verbal and/or written response.* Avoid questions that can be answered with yes or no or by pointing.

> *Example*: For *Goodnight Moon*
> a. Tell where the mouse is using these words:
>
>   in   on   under   on top of   in the corner   right   left
> b. How do you say "Goodnight" in your family?
> c. What would you say "Goodnight" to if you were sleeping in this room?

4. *Provide materials and necessary vocabulary lists to make a simple picture book on a related theme.* Allow students to choose, if possible, or pick a theme related to classroom content.

   ▱ Example:

     a. Using *Goodnight Moon* as a model, make a picture book for "Good morning, Sun." How would the mouse appear in different parts of the house in the morning at daybreak?

     b. For *Bread, Bread, Bread,* compose a picture book describing different soups, or pasta, or desserts.

     c. To expand on the pattern of *Ten, Nine, Eight,* illustrate a math facts book for "Twenty, Nineteen, Eighteen" or "Ten plus Nine, Nine plus Nine, etc."

5. *For students who can write in another language, encourage them to write "bilingual" picture books to share with other students.* Although generally it makes sense to encourage new learners to use a single language at a time, making picture books allows enough time for students to make the mental switch while writing and illustrating. Actually, texts with words of a different language interspersed have been used successfully to build a scaffold for learning, especially if the different words are illustrated or if the meaning can be inferred from the context. Students learning English can make such books interspersing vocabulary and phrases from their first language for their native-English-speaking peers. When students feel confident about their pronunciation and fluency with English, encourage them to read their books aloud to others and "teach" the words they have interspersed. An alternative exercise is to specify that the inserted terms be prepositional phrases or nouns or any other appropriate class of words.

PICTURE BOOKS FOR OLDER CHILDREN AND ADULTS

Fortunately, picture books at all levels of intellectual and artistic sophistication are available. These are good for older beginners.

The accomplishment of reading a whole book, especially one that contains wit beyond the silliness or simplicity that Americans call "childish," provides a motivating boost to the fragile egos of most people who are facing the daunting task of learning English. Suggest that books for children are a good way to reminisce; this approach will acknowledge the maturity and experience of older youth and adults.

1. Chris Van Allsburg's *The Z Was Zapped: A Play in Twenty-six Acts* is an ABC book for the sophisticated wit of older teens and adults. Twenty-six pages of simple sentences, each describing a terrible mishap and vividly illustrated in black-and-white engravings, provide a good way to stretch vocabulary. This is great fun for sardonic minds.

 Exercises:

a. Introduce a different letter (or two) in each class, reviewing preceding sentences until the whole book is finished. After the teacher reads aloud to model correct pronunciation, students should repeat the sentences aloud two or three times. Explain the quirky vocabulary, repeat, and move on. Although the vocabulary is quirky, beginners are practicing sentence patterns and pronunciation as well as learning unusual new words that they can use to impress others.

b. For creative students who want to expand their vocabulary, challenge them to write their own sentences, using an English-language dictionary. This imaginative exercise should be done outside of class or tutoring time, as it is time-consuming.

2. Another source of delightful picture reading is the popular series by Ludwig Bemelmans. *Madeline's Rescue* presents a rhyming melodrama of Miss Clavel and the twelve young girls in her charge, led by the spirited Madeline. The recent film, *Madeline: Lost in Paris*, makes this book an attractive choice for many teens and

young adults. For the most part, the detailed illustrations closely support the text, and the rhyme moves the story along quickly. The setting in a Paris boarding school is a good basis for comparison with modern schooling for females. Other books in the *Madeline* series are almost as good.

 Exercises:

1. The number of details makes this book a good choice for exercises that check for comprehension by sequencing sentences.

2. A crossword puzzle matching events with details can be used to review meaning and check for comprehension.

3. The clever rhymes are an excellent choice for choral reading or for memorizing and reciting to an audience.

Bemelmans' *Rosebud*, about a rabbit who tricks a whale and an elephant into making fools of themselves, has fairly simple vocabulary, some repetition, and a worldly sense of wit by the author of the *Madeline* series.

3. *Zachary's Ball* by Matt Tavares describes a boy's reminiscence of catching a baseball in Boston's Fenway Park and imagining himself part of the game. The tone is adult but not unsuitable for younger readers, and the black-and-white drawings are photographic in detail. This sports romance captures the nostalgic tone of baseball before Astroturf.

 Exercises:

1. Use this story to introduce biographies of sports stars.

2. For intermediate students, ask for verbal and then written responses to one of the following prompts. Provide vocabulary as needed.

   a. Describe an experience that has given you or a friend a similar thrill.

   b. Retell this story substituting a different sport.

4. Maurice Sendak's *Where the Wild Things Are* is a classic delight for readers of all ages. Although the text is not completely supported by the illustrations, the psychology of anger is universal enough to make this book easy to comprehend. Sendak's sophisticated drawings can be analyzed as art, especially for older teens and young adults, and his text is poetic: "the walls become the world all around."

🚲 *Exercises:*

1. After reading together, as described in chapter 3, discuss the disciplinary practice of "being sent to your room" as an American custom. Compare with other methods of dealing with an unhappy or troublesome child.

2. Provide materials and vocabulary lists to make simple picture books about handling anger or frustration. Younger students may need help in explaining or clarifying their concepts in concrete language.

3. Identify the various sentence patterns (simple, compound, complex). Ask students to write their own sentences, using these as models.

4. Sendak's work has been censored for several reasons, especially his candor in portraying a child's passions and desires. Collect other Sendak works and discuss the reasons for censorship. Sendak's *In the Night Kitchen* has very little text, but its cartoon nude boy, the Three Stooges, and the Milky Way are subjects for older teens and adults to discuss.

5. Another controversial book is Laura Krauss Melmed's *I Love You as Much*. The theme of a mother's love and its unorthodox portrayal makes this book more suitable for teens and adults, who can understand deep feelings and tolerate sentimentality, than for older children and teens. It could be paired with Margaret Wise Brown's *The Runaway Bunny* for a fascinating discussion about the nature of the parent-child bond in different cultures.

Exercises:

1. For beginners, the repetition of the phrase "I love you as much as a____" provides an easily learned example of the use of similes, and the phrase "said the mother" models the correct way of integrating and punctuating a quotation. Using this refrain as a model, ask students to create their own sentences aloud, and then in writing. Have the students share their written sentences with the class.

2. Review the names of animals mentioned, and discuss the illustrations that show the appropriate geographic context for each. Introduce related vocabulary.

3. Ask students to rewrite the text, using other verbs and adjectives:

> "I can run as fast as . . ."
> "I sing as loud as . . ."
> "I am as big as . . ."

6. Although many fractured fairy tales depend on a fair amount of cultural background knowledge, Jon Scieszka's *The True Story of the Three Little Pigs* seems to be an exception. This version of the traditional tale uses the kind of language that people actually use when they are telling each other stories, but in English that is grammatically correct. The humor and supporting pictures make this accessible even to beginning and intermediate-level students who are motivated by the informal tone and contemporary wit. Suitable for readers of all ages who have any familiarity with the original folktale, this book will bear rereading periodically until all the jokes are understood.

Exercises:

1. Some of the expressions Scieszka uses may need extra explanation:

> "dead as a doornail" "rude little porker" "jazzed up the story" "the brains of the family" "I was framed"

Ask students to find expressions with similar meaning in their own language and help them translate into English.

2. Students can read other versions of this tale and compare them.

WORDLESS PICTURE BOOKS

To encourage free speech and creativity, use picture books without text. Provide a list of vocabulary and phrases to use, and let new learners narrate the story. This ad-lib storytelling, using the captivating prompt of such a book, is fun to do as a small group activity.

David Wiesner's *Tuesday* is a funny fantasy in beautifully drawn pictures about frogs whose lilypads suddenly become magic carpets one Tuesday night. Only one frog doesn't seem to enjoy the ride! This book is suitable for all ages.

Exercises:

1. Count the frogs on each page.

2. After discussing and listing useful vocabulary, ask students to select a page and describe all that they can see, first aloud and then in writing. This would also be good for work in pairs or small groups.

3. Explain the joke at the end of the book when, a week later, pigs fly. Begin a collection of expressions meaning "never," such as "in a blue moon."

David Wiesner has written two other wordless books suitable for older readers: *June 29, 1999* and *Sector 7*. The first is similar to *Tuesday*, with a different theme but with a similar joke. The second is a fantasy about clouds, the Empire State Building in New York City, and a central station labeled Sector 7. It has a friendly tone and is cuter than *Tuesday*, but certainly not saccharine. More for older children and adults, this fantasy could spark discussion about the corporate world, bureaucracy, and control of the world's weather.

So many great picture books are available now that it is difficult to end this chapter. Any reluctance of older learners to use books that seem childlike should disappear once they realize how quickly and efficiently they are learning. Using picture books in conjunction with more traditional workbooks often reassures students who need a tighter structure to feel that they are progressing. Others will react more favorably to nonfiction picture books, many of which are mentioned in the following chapters. Most students appreciate the progress they can make in reading, saying, discussing, and writing new language when their understanding is stimulated and buttressed by illustrations.

CHAPTER 5

Teaching History

ALTHOUGH MOST STUDENTS could benefit from learning both North American and world history from the many excellent factual resources written for children and young adults, foreign students especially need the fuller context that good historical fiction provides, as well as the clear explanations and extra information of nonfiction written for children and young adults. An increasing number of excellent nonfiction works with colorful, detailed, and historically accurate illustrations are available for young readers.

Historical time is difficult for all young readers to conceive, just as are distances and geographical size. These concepts may be easier for children who have experienced living in a foreign country with different customs and language. Students who have memories of places outside the United States may comprehend historical events and geography more deeply than students who have not traveled. Some may even be personally aware of the relative poverty and dangerous political situations that have driven many immigrants to this country from its inception.

On the other hand, the value of remembering the past may be less obvious to foreign students than it is to Americans, who experience new technology and new inventions before most of the rest of the world. Many families who come to the United States want to forget their pasts, so studying history may seem only marginally important. Remind students—both native English speakers and ESL—that our present is the sum of all past moments, and that by studying the past we come to understand the complexities of the present.

Learning a large body of new information such as American history is like a dance in which one is first caught up in the swirl of the overall picture and then increasingly intrigued by the details. Without a timeline and a map, the individual events float in a vacuum, unrelated to each other, but maps and time lines are hard to remember without the individual stories to anchor places and times. Students who are struggling with English need to practice the language of both the large picture and the individual stories before they can express their understanding of history.

THE BIG PICTURE

A good introduction to the broad concept of history and its general sequence is in *What Your First Grader Needs to Know*, the first volume of E. D. Hirsch's Core Knowledge Series. This collection of books, one for each grade level, was designed as a guidebook to the "commonly shared knowledge" of educated people. Although this project is controversial, especially its underlying assumption that all people in the United States should share a common curriculum, the volumes of this series are useful as an organized and accessible introduction to the subject, with short passages written in a simple, direct style.

Letting each student read a single short passage aloud will introduce at least the vocabulary of history even to young students just learning English. After each passage, the idea or information can be reinforced with appropriate-level picture books or fictional accounts. Like many young learners, these children will grasp only vague outlines of historical events and their meanings, but these outlines will form the basis for more specific learning later. For students with more advanced language skills, more than one passage can be introduced at a sitting.

Older students with basic skills in English but with more mature intelligence may be slightly offended at the simplified information or the slightly patronizing tone that Hirsch uses in his volume for first graders, a tone that is used in many books written for primary students and that many consider appropriate for young children in our culture. Already struggling to cope with the inevitable feelings of ineptness when trying to learn a new language that their age-level peers already know, older learners may feel defensive. Since the Core Knowledge Series presents history chronologically without repeating facts in subsequent volumes, it might be wise to summarize the information of early books in a more age-appropriate tone or use another source for an overview of world history to avoid inadvertently insulting these new students.

In volumes aimed at fourth grade and above, the tone is more appropriate for older students and even adults; the series presents increasingly detailed information and complex concepts in clear, forthright language.

Another useful nonfiction resource is *The Usborne Book of World History: A Children's Encyclopedia of History* by Anne Millard and Patricia Vanags. This is a wonderful resource for all ages, reviewing both the general sequence of world history and the mundane texture of life. Detailed colored drawings trace the lives of ordinary people and also portray famous leaders and events. Each double page holds about nine scenes, either separated into frames or forming parts of a large overall picture; the accompanying text is direct, simple, and brief— perfect for struggling readers. The layout and tone of this volume is suitable for all ages. A two-page time chart at the end of the book shows the relationship of key events in various parts of the world up to the beginning of the twenty-first century. As with most summaries of world history, the emphasis is on European and U.S. history, though this book does include chapters about the sweep of events on other continents. Fifty-five sections are spread over 190 pages, and each page contains several paragraphs of information, arranged like captions under the pictures. Readers who consider themselves beyond the beginning level yet are still struggling with English may not realize how much information is covered by the brief text, and may need to be reassured that they are accomplishing more than they realize when they read just a few pages.

Some encyclopedias that are limited in scope nonetheless cover a range of touchstone figures for understanding a span of history.

Johanna Johnston's *They Led the Way: 14 American Women* marks the chronology of U.S. history with stories of female figures from Mistress Anne Hutchinson, who was banished from the Massachusetts colony for preaching, to Carrie Chapman Catt, who worked to help American women achieve the right to vote in 1920. Chapters of about eight pages review these lives using easy-to-read dialogue and language, in a tone that would be reassuringly simple for beginning readers. For more sophisticated readers, *Cool Women: The Thinking Girl's Guide to the Hippest Women in History* uses a jazzy layout of photos, quotes, and sidebars to introduce famous women from all over the globe, from Cleopatra of Egypt to Evita of Argentina. While the text is not particularly basic, it is well supported by the illustrations.

Many other encyclopedic works are too overwhelming and dense to use with students who are already struggling with English. However, books containing labeled pictures are useful as classroom resources for special occasions and research projects. One example is *The Dorling-Kindersley History of the World* by Plantagenet Somerset Fry. More comprehensive than Usborne's history, this hefty volume of 384 pages of glossy photographs and small print contains time lines, statistics, lists, and specific dates. Like similar books, its best use is as a resource for review and extension. Since ESL students are learning the language as well as the information, they can benefit from the repetition and reinforcement that these books provide.

BIG PICTURE EXERCISES

1. *An illustrated time line in the classroom will help all students keep historical sequence straight.* Create a time line large enough to display on a wall, and make smaller copies for the students' individual use. Divide the time line into units of fifty years, except for the twentieth century, which is most often divided into decades. Use sticky notes or colored dots to situate biographies, historical fiction, and

nonfiction on the time line. Encourage students to use their own copies of a time line to track their own learning and reading about histories of their favorite subjects, as well as general history. Include events from students' home areas whenever possible.

2. *Keep a large world map available and collect magazine illustrations and photos of different types of geography.* Ask students to match the pictures with regions on the map. Repeat this exercise regularly to fix mental images of various areas with their names.

3. *Help students make a scrapbook with a section for each continent, a page for major regions, and a half page for each country or for each state in the United States.* As students learn, they can list interesting facts and resources in the appropriate section. Have the students share notebooks often to allow them to learn from each other's work and to motivate good work.

The overall sweep and flow of historical time and geographical place is too abstract to hold most people's attention without detailed examples that we can tie to our personal experiences. Stories of individual personalities, in places we can visualize, with motivations we can feel, help us comprehend the complex networks of people and events behind the terms and famous names we memorize. The books named below, a small sampling of the many fine works available in most libraries, are chosen to show what kind of criteria can be used to engage ESL learners in an imaginative revisiting of history.

The Legend of Mackinac Island by Kathy-jo Wargin, a brightly painted book, retells the Native American legend of how Mackinac Island in Michigan was created from the back of a turtle. The quietly respectful tone is suitable for adults and teens with low-intermediate-level proficiency; the thirty pages of text are easy to read and well illustrated.

🚲 *Exercises:*

1. Use this and similar books to provide touch points for beginning work with maps. Provide a world map and a

globe as well as a map of the United States to indicate the relative location of Michigan. Introduce words indicating direction, weather, and relative distances. Make comparisons and contrasts between Michigan and the ESL students' countries of origin with regard to geographic setting, weather, size, and ethnic groups. Encourage conversations among other students that lead to identifying various places on the maps and globe.

2. Discuss the differences between "legend" and "history" as "true" explanations about the past; both kinds of truth may be valid, one an analysis of written and observable evidence and the other embedded in language symbolic of more spiritual truths.

In George Ella Lyon's *Who Came Down that Road?,* a mother and child imagine the many people who have traveled down a single route in front of a young boy's house in rural Kentucky. Beginning with the mammoths and other beasts of the Stone Age, and progressing through human history in North America from the indigenous tribes who hunted and traveled west, to frontiersmen and soldiers of the Civil War, Lyon traces the outlines of U.S. history in broad strokes.

For older students as well as younger readers, *A Street through Time: A 12,000 Year Walk through History* by Anne Millard illustrates the changes over time of a site somewhere in Europe or England from 10,000 B.C. to the present. Canoes become sailboats, steamships, and eventually gasoline-powered vessels. The hill in the background is fortified with a bulwark that develops into a castle that eventually erodes into ruins. People of all economic and social levels participate in the scenes portrayed in detailed drawings along this road; business and play for the rich and the poor, the old and the young, are included in this panoramic stroll through the ages. As a bonus, a young character named Henry Hyde is portrayed on each of the twelve pages, encouraging a careful perusal to find him.

🚲 *Exercises:*

1. Ask students first to tell about and then to write about a place they know well that has changed. Using either book as a model, select four or five places in different geographical areas, and trace probable changes that have occurred over the centuries in each of those sites.

2. Ask student or adult volunteers to compose similar books to prepare students for studying the places mentioned in the school curriculum. Students can illustrate these texts after some research in the historic encyclopedias mentioned above to indicate comprehension.

3. Rewrite several passages from Lyon's book in a different tense, changing the verbs accordingly.

4. Expand the vocabulary labels in Millard's book into whole sentences or short passages imagining what individual characters in the pictures are thinking.

SELECTING HISTORICAL LITERATURE

Most historical fiction is aimed at students of middle school age and older, but more short picture books dealing with history have recently been published for younger readers. Unfortunately, very little of this literature reaches beyond the boundaries of U.S. history, with the exception of encyclopedias and the many recent books about the World War II Holocaust in Europe. As publishers react to state and regional "standards of learning" curricula, more books about other histories are becoming available.

Whether fictional or factual, historical literature for new learners of English should:

1. Describe and illustrate historical events accurately in authentic settings;
2. Portray realistic characters that are easy to care about;

3. Avoid stereotypical generalizations;
4. Use straightforward language that presents the story clearly, yet succinctly;
5. Avoid the use of heavy dialect and complex or indirect language.

Resources for good historical literature can be obtained at low cost from the National Council for the Social Studies (3501 Newark St. NW, Washington, DC 20016; Tel. 202-966-7840). For readers who are still straining to comprehend English text, first choose books with small amounts of text to let them learn the general outline of the historical period before reading further about the same subjects in books with longer text sections. Repetition of the same material in different words will help set the subject in their memories and deepen their understanding. Encourage readers to alternate between researching a subject in the surveys and encyclopedias mentioned above and reading about particular events and characters in books similar to those discussed in the following sections. Learning a wide range of material seems to occur most effectively when students swing between a general overview and specific examples. Perhaps detailed knowledge about single events or characters works to firmly fasten footholds in memory for the time and place.

SEQUENCING HISTORICAL FICTION

Common sense might indicate that historical fiction should be presented chronologically, but actually most of us learn about events in bits and pieces that our minds arrange when necessary. What makes more sense with new language learners is to begin with material that is most accessible or familiar, and then arrange sequences later with the help of a time line and with cause-and-result chains. For teachers in public schools, the curriculum often dictates which parts of history must be learned at various ages.

Wendy Madgwick's *Questions and Answers: Ancient Civilizations* with clear explanatory drawings accompanied by direct, simple text, outlines the first known cultures of Egypt, Babylon, China, Celtic Britain, and the Mayan empire with gentle humor and a question-answer format. Each double-spread page identifies the relevant geography and dates, and covers the most familiar facets of each civilization. *The Medieval World* by Philip Steele focuses on the knights, castles, and other chivalric aspects of the first millennium A.D. The watercolor illustrations detail even facial expressions of the characters in this ninety-page encyclopedia. More inclusive but also more challenging for a new learner is the cartoon book *Adventures in the Middle Ages* by Linda Bailey and Bill Slavin. This series is about the Binkerton twins who travel back in time to medieval times and experience adventures from the country village to the castle. The tone is cute and clever but informative too.

A good resource to provide an overview of American history either as an introduction or as a review is the book by Cheryl Harness, *Remember the Ladies*: *100 Great American Women*. Two or three sentences describe each of the many women who contributed to American history. This annotated list is illustrated with breezy drawings and includes references to many other prominent names and events.

THEMATIC READING

For low-intermediate or young readers, reading several works on a single theme reinforces vocabulary and comprehension of the historical context to lead them toward an in-depth analysis of a longer work. Whenever possible, begin with picture books that illustrate the time period and geographical area before progressing to longer works. A unit about the American Revolution might begin with Louise Borden's *Sleds on Boston Common*. The harbor in Boston is closed and British soldiers are in the way of Henry's favorite sled run. When Henry politely protests to General Gage, the leader admires his spunk and has the soldiers clear the way for the boys to sled. The brightly colored sketches support the text; both text and illustrations describe the tensions between the citizens of Boston and the British that eventually lead to the American Revolution. Another helpful text is Ann Turner's short book *Katie's Trunk*, which depicts the fear of the general public toward the rabble-rousing Patriots. Follow with brief biographies of the major players like Jean Fritz's *And Then What Happened, Paul Revere?* and *Will You Sign Here, John Hancock?* to contrast the lives of a tradesman and a wealthy landowner. *Buttons for General Washington* by Peter and Connie Roop tells the story of a young boy sent on a dangerous mission to deliver buttons with messages encoded in them to the Revolutionary soldiers. The text is simple and presented in large print, with accompanying illustrations to aid young readers. Carol Greene's *Thomas Jefferson: Author, Inventor, President* also uses large print and short simple sentence patterns, but the accompanying photographs and contemporary drawings provide quite sophisticated information. Robert Lawson's delightful story is summarized by its title, the lengthiest sentence in the book's 152 pages: *Mr. Revere and I, Being an Account of Certain Episodes in the Career of Paul Revere, Esq. as Recently Revealed by his Horse, Scheherazade, Late Pride of His Royal Majesty's 14th Regiment of Foot, Set Down and Embellished with Numerous Drawings by Robert Lawson*. This is the story of the Boston uprising from the viewpoint of a British horse. Initially this narrator expresses no sympathy for the provincial outpost with all of its churches and none of London's glamour. The style of his discourse, which at first matches his disdain, becomes more ingenuous as time passes and he becomes caught up in the excitement of Paul Revere's mission. A natural contrast is Lawson's book of the same year: *Ben and Me: A New and Astonishing Life of Benjamin Franklin as Written by his Good Mouse, Amos, Lately Discovered, Edited and Illustrated by Robert Lawson*. Another lighthearted but historically accurate book that shows how the American Revolution was viewed from abroad is Jean Fritz's *Can't You Make Them Behave, King George?* King George is depicted as a scholarly and good-hearted young man who considered the colonists with the same puzzlement as did most of his subjects. Although many newer books about the American Revolution with bright and colored illustrations are available, the text is often so dense with information that the story becomes buried. New readers of English may not be able to absorb so many details as they must focus on decoding the shape of the plot and differentiating among the main characters.

My Brother Sam Is Dead by James and Christopher Collier is longer, a 210-page classic of young adult historical fiction that illustrates the courage necessary to rebel against the traditional strength of Great Britain. It would be a good read-aloud for intermediate-level learners. Excited about the first skirmish between the British soldiers and the rebels, Sam returns to his home, a tavern in Connecticut owned and run by his loyalist father, who remembers the horrors of the French and Indian War too vividly to want to see any violence again. Narrated by younger brother Tim, this novel analyzes the many reasons that law-abiding British citizens would feel compelled to rebel: Sam likes the excitement, his father resents the impositions on his livelihood, and Tim is drawn in by loyalties to his family and friends. The impact of war on ordinary families is portrayed in all of its complexity and tragedy. Many other excellent books are available for younger readers to compare and contrast different attitudes toward the war. The more that new learners are exposed to language and information about an important world-changing event, the more they learn the vocabulary, the issues, and the content of the school subject called "history."

 Exercises:

1. On a simple time line, list the main events that led up to the American Revolution, and make it available to listeners and readers. Together, fill in the details as they are mentioned in the readings. Each student can write one or more small passages describing an event or person, and then tack it up in appropriate places on the time line.

2. Use pictures, simple explanations, and maps to clarify the terms "lobsterback," "Yankee," and "New England" as they were used in 1775. Explain that colonists ate lobsters more out of necessity than preference, and that many early settlers were grateful for the British army's protection against the French, Indians, pirates, Spanish, and other forces who wanted to claim some of the resources and opportunities promised in this new land.

3. Try to compare the events in the readings with the events in the students' homelands. For beginning or younger students, elicit help from parents or older students who may have time to research these histories by Internet.

Fever 1793 by Laurie Halse Anderson uses simple language to describe the life of a middle-class teenaged girl in Philadelphia from August to December 1793. One of the many yellow fever plagues threatens first a neighboring servant girl, and then her own mother. This exciting adventure brings to life many historical verities about Revolutionary America that get buried in the military events: The Free African Society, the French influence, the debate about medical practices, and the daily routines of cooking, cleaning, and childcare.

The Clock by James and Christopher Collier, also about an adolescent girl in troubled times, is similar in length and tone. The economic depression of the 1830s and her father's ill-fated investments mean that our heroine must go to work in a wool factory. The death of a friend with a bad leg and the schemes of her boss make this book an exciting adventure and a good way for beginning readers at the low intermediate proficiency level to learn about the effects of the Industrial Revolution on rural America.

At ninety-two pages Gary Paulsen's *Nightjohn* is the right length for readers at the low intermediate level, and the life-threatening plot situation is highly motivating. The portrayal of slavery is brutally honest, but the nonstandard English dialect is not the language considered acceptable in most schoolwork. On the other hand, readers familiar with street language will have no trouble understanding the text. Many of the scenes are raw and violent, but mature readers will appreciate the hero's tough and courageous intelligence in teaching his fellow slaves to read, even under the threat of death. After finishing this book, some students may want to hear at least part of Paulsen's longer sequel, *Sarny,* read aloud.

Another choice for this type of reader could be Karen Hesse's *Out of the Dust*. With 125 pages of brief text arranged like poems with lots of white space, this book is less daunting than longer texts. The story is set in Oklahoma, beginning in the winter of 1934, when many Americans were weathering the economic depression; drought and dust storms that plagued much of the Midwest drove many further into poverty and some out of their minds. Many left their homes to wander toward California, looking for work and a new life. Hesse paints a vivid picture of this era from the viewpoint of a young girl, Red, who tells her story in short, flat sentences, struck bold with details and metaphors so apt that the book is almost physically painful to read. Indeed, while the simple vocabulary and spare grammar would seem perfect for a new language learner, the directness of the images may be too strong for a sensitive reader.

The book begins with a birth, as the mother, "bare-bottomed" and barefooted, drops her only living child on the wood floor, swept clean. Later, the narrator burns her mother raw in an accident, injuring her own hands as she saves her; her father drinks his pain away as his wife lies dying. The book is strong, but a true picture of a painful time in history. It would be a good alternative to Steinbeck's *The Grapes of Wrath* and *Of Mice and Men* or a companion to either film.

Another cruel point in recent history is the Holocaust of World War II. Although most historical literature published for young readers focuses on American history, this almost unbearable period is an exception. David Adler's *Hilde and Eli: Children of the Holocaust* uses simple text supported by powerful illustrations to tell the dramatic story of two children caught up in the tragic web of World War II in a format accessible to low-intermediate-level readers.

An appropriate follow-up would be Lois Lowry's *Number the Stars,* which relates how a young girl and her family help their Jewish neighbors. This fascinating adventure is historically accurate in its description of some of the ploys used to thwart the Nazis' plans for extermination of all Jews, yet also contains touching portraits of people of all ages. It is suitable for male and female readers, young and adult. Also see *Surviving Hitler: A Boy in the Nazi Death Camps* by Andrea Warren for a gripping story very simply told.

Longer well-written historical fiction provides older readers an opportunity to know places, events, and characters in depth, in the same way as people make friends out of mere acquaintances and homes out of places. Longer novels also give readers a chance to get used to the author's individual style and vocabulary. For beginning learners of English, listening to most of each chapter while reading along provides good practice in matching print to sound; the reader's intonation will indicate the general meaning or emotional tone and help stretch comprehension of vocabulary. Whenever possible, every student should practice output—speech and writing, even when it is rote repetition and copying. Advanced language learners can participate more and more, each time the novel is repeated, on audiotape or by silent reading.

Remember that the longer time spent with a novel-length book is not wasted. Students need the opportunity to learn language thoroughly as much as they need variety of input, and many don't have that chance for most of each day. While students may seem to understand everything that is going on, many have become more adept at fitting in socially than grappling with all the informational details. Repeated reading lets students learn both the language and the content material in layers. First, they establish the general outline or gist of the story, then fill in the sequence and cause-and-effect relationships, and finally grasp the details and nuances of the language.

SERIES BOOKS

In recent years, publishers have been issuing series of historical fiction. When students become involved in reading a series of similar books, they absorb the language patterns and the conventions of plot, character, and sequence of the genre, and improve their reading fluency. Often series become popular with a group of readers, inspiring discussion about the characters and events; collecting and reading the books in the series becomes a socializing force as well as a way of learning about history. The language in these series often represents a modern version of the historical dialect; some nonstandard phrases and words are scattered throughout, but they do not dominate. They would be accessible to highly motivated readers at the intermediate and advanced levels, but frustrating for readers who need shorter sentences, a larger number of supporting illustrations, and more repetitive language.

Scholastic's *Dear America* series is written in diary form by fictional characters who find themselves immersed in events which later become known as turning points in U.S. history. The series is excellent; many of the volumes are written by highly acclaimed authors and depict the daily texture of life for young people, including references to chores, education, clothes, courtship, and recreation. Maps, time lines, and, when possible, photos of the era help the reader tie each story to the academic study of history.

Recently, Scholastic has added a similar series that introduces characters outside American history. Each of the *Royal Diaries* tells the story of a princess. Included are Anastasia of Russia, Elizabeth of England, Njanga of Africa, and Kuiliana of Hawaii. *Anastasia: The Last Grand Duchess* by Carolyn Meyer includes a glossary of characters, a family chart, a few photographs, and a brief summary of Russian history of the time.

The *American Girls Collection*, aimed at female readers from the age of seven to twelve, introduces a series of fictional girls who represent different ethnic groups at various points in American history.

The accompanying dolls, crafts, specialized booklets, and other study aids inspire a trend in some circles that can be quite a motivation for some readers, but the long chapters, complex language, and slow-moving stories can be difficult for new learners of English. These volumes do paint vivid pictures of various times in American history.

Other series, *American Adventures* and *My Name Is America,* are aimed at male readers. These novel-length books with short chapters focus more on physical details than on the emotional responses of the characters. Events happen quickly; suspense is the overriding tone. *American Diaries* by Kathleen Duey includes books written from the viewpoint of both male and female fictional characters from various historical periods. Longer and more descriptive, some of these contain dialectic expressions and styles of speech that may deter struggling readers. The *Coming to America* series about immigration could spark discussion about modern methods of coming to North America; these too tend to have longer chapters and more sophisticated language than previously mentioned novels. Individual readers will become so wrapped up in learning about a character or events that mirror their own experiences that they quickly overcome these difficulties.

MULTICULTURAL HISTORY

Until recently, much of the history learned in schools was the story of the mainstream, highlighting the events and leaders valued by the dominant culture. Now history textbooks and lessons try to include all cultural groups, as well as all age groups and both sexes. For new learners of English whose attention span is already stretched by learning new language along with new content, the question arises of how much to include.

One method is to indicate on a wall chart or a time line the relative population involved in each event, or the event's relative impact on central government and history. Students can trace the traditional direction of "history" as measured by most assessment packages, or they can delve into non-mainstream events as their language learning allows. Does this perpetuate the marginalizing of people and events not traditionally recognized as dominant? Of course it does, but standardized testing standardizes learning.

In reality, by naming non-traditional events and giving access to some resources about them, teachers enable students to pursue those figures and events which catch their interest, either because they share similar stories and cultures, or just "because." Some students may be motivated by these resources to read beyond the assignments necessary to succeed in class. Multicultural books, including histories, are described in chapter 7.

BIOGRAPHIES

The same principle applies to the many wonderful biographies that are written for young people: An excellent reinforcement of information about historical context for many readers, they will be less useful (or attractive) to readers who expend a great effort simply to comprehend the gist of a story. On the other hand, some biographies may inspire readers who have a particular interest in learning about an individual. Even biographies about sports stars contain background information that strengthens readers' understanding about historical context. Allowing students choice and time to read and write about the shaping of history — both personal and cultural — is a powerful motivator to learning.

CHAPTER 6

Teaching Math and Science

FOR MOST NEW ENGLISH LANGUAGE LEARNERS, measures of academic achievement show that they score lower in math and science than native-born students. One explanation is that the majority of their formal learning is focused on reading and language arts materials rather than on math and science. However, there is no logical or pedagogical reason to avoid these content areas. Each has its own vocabulary and set of rules, but these are no more difficult than learning the set of words and phrases and cultural expectations of eating at various types of restaurants.

People learn about what they see and hear when they can see the connections to something they already know. Many books written for young people use pictures or references to daily life that make connections between familiar objects and terms and more sophisticated concepts of math and science.

The first step in making math and science accessible is matching the appropriate vocabulary with the basic materials and concepts of each content area. In this chapter, some ideas for using both fiction and nonfiction written for young readers will help the teacher provide the extra language support necessary for nonnative speakers of English.

MATH

In contrast to most school systems in the United States, many schools in other countries emphasize science and math at the elementary and middle school levels as much as or more than reading and literature.

It makes logical sense that math would be easier for immigrants because it does not seem so dependent on knowing English, and for some, this proves to be true. However, do remember that numbers and simple math terms are so familiar to native speakers that we tend to rattle them off, without being conscious of listeners who may be struggling to follow along and react appropriately. We say the names of numbers just as we say our own names, swallowing the last syllables and slurring vowels without careful enunciation.

Using picture books with numbers helps students to become just as familiar with the names of numbers in their various combinations. Many picture counting books with clever themes and colorful illustrations are available in the children's section of libraries and bookstores. Select several to use for daily drills for beginning and even low intermediate students; snazzy and sophisticated selections will attract readers who may otherwise feel patronized by the use of children's books. At the end of several sessions, divert the focus by asking students to vote on the best illustrations or the most useful. The purpose is for students to be able to remember and use numbers automatically.

For beginning readers, one good number book is Molly Bang's *Ten, Nine, Eight*. Bright pictures make it fun. For older readers, the counting series by Jim Haskins combines counting with geography, history, and other languages. Haskins's *Counting Your Way through Africa* includes numbers in Swahili, but also in English. Each page features interesting facts about a country as well as its money and information about the geography of the continent, its political systems, trade, music, dances, and other art forms. The text is brief and simply formatted. Other volumes provide an overview of the Arab world (1987), China (1987), Russia (1987), India (1990), Greece (1996), and Brazil (1996).

One Grain of Rice: A Mathematical Folktale by Demi demonstrates the exponential power of doubling a number in the form of a story about a young girl who tricks a raja into rewarding her for her honesty by giving her twice as much rice as the previous day for thirty days. From one grain of rice, her stockpile grows to more than a billion grains, enough to feed all the hungry people, even the raja. The gorgeous artwork clearly illustrates the short text passages, using fold-out pages to allow for pictures of 256 elephants who carry the 536,870,912 grains of rice on the final day. The numbers are both spelled out in words and written numerically in a convenient chart at the end of the book, providing a great opportunity for practice in reading and saying larger numbers, as well as comprehending their magnitude. For low intermediate readers, this also introduces simple vocabulary about India, useful in geography: the animals that carry the rice include monkeys, tigers, elephants, and Brahma bulls, all clearly illustrated.

After learning to recognize easily and quickly, the sounds and sight of numbers and their adjectival forms ("first," "second," etc.) students need to learn the vocabulary of computations, some of which they may already know how to do. Once students can say, read, and understand the names of numbers consecutively, they should practice them in random order and in various combinations such as in simple computations. Partners can make this into a game by throwing dice to select numbers to add, subtract, divide, and multiply.

The closely worded logic of word problems can be particularly difficult for new learners of English until they master the names of computations and concepts, so it is important to practice these terms and concepts until they become automatic. Several fictional books for children incorporate simple math in their plots. These provide practice in logic, language, and math all at the same time.

Mitsumasa Anno's *Magic Seeds* teaches multiplication by observing a lazy farmer get lucky with magic seeds that keep producing plants with more seeds, and so forth. Readers also get practice in other math operations as the plot turns.

Pat Hutchins's *The Doorbell Rang* uses a story about sharing a plate of twelve cookies among an increasing number of children to illustrate the basic principles of division. Joan Glazer recommends this text as a good resource for teaching math.

Norton Juster's *The Dot and the Line: A Romance in Lower Mathematics* is a charming demonstration of the transformation of a straight line into a fascinating array of angles. As its title suggests, the geometric possibilities are not so much explained in dry academic fashion as woven into a story of passionate love. The eighty pages contain few words, but students will find it hard to forget the vocabulary and concepts of simple geometry after enjoying this story. This book is especially suitable for older students.

For math, providing a chart with arithmetic terms illustrated by concrete examples is relatively easy. A word list with synonyms and signs that indicate addition, subtraction, multiplication, and division provides a basis for diagnostic assessment. Don't forget the idiomatic terms and phrases that may seem simple to natives: "and," "take away, took away," "how many are left," "times," and "goes into" (often pronounced "gazinta"). Besides charts and posters, some books like those discussed below demonstrate math language in alternate ways.

Math Curse by Jon Scieszka with twenty-five pages of text introduces much of the language and logic of word problems with a healing dash of humor. Cursed by her teacher's announcement that most problems can be solved by math, the young narrator describes a whole day of quandaries in mathematical language. The sophisticated wit makes this suitable for all ages, including adults. Allow time and opportunity to examine the book's end pieces and its covers, which tease students with more math language and puns. The dedication reads, "If the sum of my nieces and nephews equals 15, and their product equals 54, and I have more nephews than nieces. . . ." Native-English-speaking students will enjoy explaining the puns expressed in math symbols, but do warn them to avoid overloading the attention span of beginning students. This would be a good book to assign for home reading and extended study so that students can review the many mathematical symbols introduced in the book.

🚲 Exercises:

1. Make up math "problems" based on familiar situations for each other to solve. Ask an understanding native speaker

to edit kindly for grammar, spelling, and idiomatic expressions to prevent undue embarrassment.

2. Pair a student with advanced language skills or a native speaker with an intermediate-level ESL student to research, write, and illustrate a "course" book for other subjects with specialized vocabularies such as chemistry, physics, geography, computer science, or grammar. As an introduction to a new subject, provide a list of vocabulary, formulas, concepts, and other information to be included, as well as definite deadlines.

Especially in a subject like math in which native speakers are sometimes as unsure of their work, a contest or a "book fair" in which partners read and review the work of other people (kindly, noting two strengths to every suggestion for improvement) might motivate students even more than the impulse to entertain.

My First Math Book by David and Wendy Clemson is an attractive glossy book with photographed illustrations to help explain mathematical symbols, shapes, and other concepts. The text is sparse and simple. A bonus is the Spanish translation by Maria Millan (Barcelona: Editorial Molino, 1994), which may be welcome for native Spanish speakers or, just as important, help native English speakers learn terms in the language of their Spanish-speaking peers.

Traditionally in the United States, teachers tend to introduce a new mathematical function by explaining the process and then asking students to practice individually on related problems. In Japan, teachers begin teaching a new concept by presenting a related problem for groups of students to solve on their own. Only after students present their solutions (or attempts) does the teacher explain the function.

Several recent exemplary programs based on NCTM (National Council of Teachers of Mathematics, 1989) standards also emphasize problem-solving of life-like situations as a way to learn math by using it. Books written for young people are sources of story problems for a variety of calculation types. For new learners of English, couching math problems in the language of a familiar story is reassuring, as it lets them focus their attention on the logic of the problem rather than the quirks of an unfamiliar situation. One example of an easy-to-read book suitable for any reader from second grade to the adult level is John Reynolds Gardiner's *Stone Fox*. Only eighty-one pages and ten chapters long, the novel is heart-warming without being sentimental or mushy. Accessible for low-intermediate-level students, the length of this novel gives readers time to know a single context, yet the plot is complex and suspenseful enough to maintain interest. Ten-year-old Willy lives with his grandfather on a Wyoming potato farm in the first half of the twentieth century. When his grandfather becomes paralyzed with depression on hearing that he will lose his farm because of unpaid taxes, Willy tries to come up with a scheme to save the farm. In the end, he succeeds and, along the way, finds plenty of opportunities to use math.

For starters, students can figure out the percentage of annual tax Willy's grandfather should have been paying, and the percentage of the penalty. Willy tries to figure out how many more potatoes he could raise and sell; the idea of expenses and profit is introduced. When Willy decides to enter his dog in a sled race, he trains along a route, and he wins by taking a shortcut over a lake. All these provide contexts for problems involving measuring distances, simple geometry, and various computations. Other subjects for discussion are the displacement of Native Americans and the power of volition, a concept discussed in the text, which is useful for anyone struggling to learn in a new language.

Marilyn Burns's books (*Math and Literature, K–3, Book One*) are collections of math problems that she finds embedded in children's classic fictions. One problem she describes in Laura Ingalls's *Little House on the Prairie* series involves Mary and Laura figuring out how to share two cookies equally between themselves and their younger sister, Carrie. Burns has also written collections for older children. Her discovery of challenging math problems in these children's classics could easily be applied to other books.

A good resource book for practicing math facts and vocabulary is Andrew King's *Math for Fun Projects*. Direct and simple in format with many useful diagrams and drawings, the language is probably too varied for low intermediate students to use themselves without the guidance of a native speaker, but the games and projects are useful both for computation drills and for hands-on illustrations of concepts. The projects begin with tips for practicing adding and subtracting, and progress through subjects as sophisticated as third-dimensional measuring and simple geometry. A glossary provides definitions of the concepts and terms demonstrated by the projects. To boost confidence and improve social skills of new learners of English, teach them some of the "tricks" so they can perform for their native peers. Let them practice the exact phrases they need to use so they can perform with ease and elan.

Mitsumasa Anno has published a collection of games suitable for clarifying and practicing mathematical concepts for new learners of English who are ready for more advanced math. *Anno's Math Games* features sets, combining, sequence, and measurement; concepts about mathematical relationships, units of measure, and the structure of matter; and finally, games about spatial dimensions and geometry, mazes, left- and right-handedness, and electrical circuits.

For older students who need to learn the basic vocabulary of math but who might feel intellectually insulted by the childish look of appropriate textbooks, Hirsch's Core Knowledge Series can provide basic facts in an adult format. The nature of these summaries written for adults who are tutoring or teaching children makes them perfect for students whose knowledge of math may exceed their ability to use the appropriate English for learning more. A quick overview of numbers can be found in *What Your First Grader Needs to Know* (pp. 236–265). Diagrams help to express each concept, and all necessary vocabulary is reviewed. Show new students with limited English the labeled diagrams, and review pronunciation. These pages can be used on subsequent meetings as flash cards, until the numbers can be read without hesitation.

The second volume, *What Your Second Grader Needs to Know* includes more advanced math (pp. 228–292), and especially useful sections on counting money and beginning word problems. The drawings and examples are clear, simple, and presented in a format suitable for older children, teens, and adults.

SCIENCE

Attractively formatted and illustrated trade books for young people about nature and other science topics brighten the shelves of every bookstore and library. Include these books in reading and language arts lessons, as suggested in the first chapters. New learners of English at the basic level can begin with picture books that introduce the concepts and vocabulary underlying the biology and chemistry they will later need. Programs that use real objects and tie scientific concepts to daily experience help reinforce the language used in texts, videos, and other educational media.

Hirsch's Core Knowledge Series, mentioned above, also reviews the range of science concepts basic to our academic system, ranging from *What Your First Grader Needs to Know* upwards beyond the sixth grade. Another general overview and introduction is *Life Sciences: Content and Learning Strategies* by Sharron Bassano, and Mary Ann Christison. These descriptions of strategies that the authors have tested out in their own classrooms include glossaries and vocabulary activities and exercises to encourage scientific thinking. Suitable for small group activities and also for individual tutoring situations, this provides the kind of support that new language learners especially need.

A program that students of all ages enjoy, mainly because it encourages the kind of social interactions and cooperative learning so helpful to new language learners, is *Math and Science: A Solution,* published by the AIMS Education Foundation. This is an experiential curriculum designed by practicing teachers that focuses on using ordinary materials and hands-on experiences to demonstrate a wide variety of scientific concepts. Introduce the main vocabulary to new language learners a few days prior to the lesson, allowing them to practice hearing and saying these terms. Use cards or a wall chart so these students can fully participate with their native-English-speaking peers. AIMS is a wonderful program for connecting life with textbook language; supplementing trade books provides a solid foundation for understanding the main topics of basic math and science. Most important, it is fun!

A SAMPLE OF SCIENCE AND NATURE BOOKS

Many nonfiction books have beautiful illustrations and photographs, but the text is positioned in large blocks of small dense print, under or opposite the illustration. More useful for new language learners are texts that use many illustrations and match them with the relevant small bit of text in a fashion similar to a picture dictionary. This allows new readers to use both the context and illustration to construct the appropriate meaning.

Using books from a series helps new language learners because, once they learn the format, they can focus on new vocabulary and information. Just as routines get automated and free up attention, texts using a similar structure and style reassure new readers because they look familiar. Below are some series and single books that use simple text and helpful patterns of illustration.

1. Plants

Ann Burkhardt's *Corn* is very easy to read with colorful illustrations, describing how corn grows and its impact around the world. It includes directions for making a corn husk wreath. The series includes similar books by the same author and illustrator about apples, potatoes, and pumpkins.

Another series about plants, *Gardens of the Earth* by Jason Cooper, uses simple large-print text and gorgeous color photographs to explore various categories of plants, each focusing on a different seasonal context. For example, the book *Trees* explains the changes of plants during autumn. Each volume of twenty-four pages has a useful glossary and an appendix about various ways of extending vocabulary that is helpful in teaching. Also available in Spanish, this series could ensure a fairly comprehensive understanding of botany as partners work together to interpret the information as fully as possible, with the help of photographs, the glossary, and the context, and with translation if necessary. *Wildlife in Danger* is a similar series about endangered animals by the same publisher, Rourke Enterprises.

Biologist Margaret Selsam and photographer Jerome Wexler teamed up to write an easy-to-read but richly informative book about plants, *The Amazing Dandelion*. The focus is on the dandelion, but the author's background as a biology teacher helps her to explain the whole process of growth, reproduction, and dissemination in great detail. The photographs are magnified, and the simple direct text explains each step, along with good-humored comments about the prolific nature of this cheerful pesky flower. The author has written similar volumes about peanuts, microbes, animal reproduction, and underwater plants and animals. These would be appropriate for mature readers with low-intermediate language proficiency.

2. Animals

Wild World of Animals, a British series published by Grisewood Dempey, has large attractive illustrations that depict the animals and plants in various geographic environments, and informative insets that add interesting details to the easy-to-read forty pages of text. One example is Michael Chinery's *Seashores*. This series, suitable for low-intermediate students and adults, includes volumes about deserts, jungles, prairies, oceans, forests, lakes and rivers, and polar regions. These books have all been translated into Spanish and published by Editorial Everest in Madrid.

Wildlife and Environmental Issues

Karen Dudley's *Bald Eagles* is suitable for intermediate ESL students. This and similar books in the series are brightly colored encyclopedias of pictures, photographs, and boxed text that describe the animal, its environmental needs and status, and traditional lore. They are useful reference books and resources for research. Other topics in the series include giant pandas, wolves, and great white sharks.

Jean Craighead George is a renowned writer of literature for young people whose books foster a profound understanding of how environmental components interrelate naturally, and how human intervention is so often destructive. The Thirteen Moon series of shorter books about events in the life cycles of various animals are well-written and informative stories. *The Moon of the Owls* portrays a great horned owl searching for a mate in the wintry nights of February. Although Jean George gives human feelings to her animals, her science is well researched and hardly romantic. George also writes novels for young readers that explore environmental issues in depth, imparting more detailed information than is available in many textbooks and embedding it in good stories with complex, unforgettable characters. The novels that would be accessible to ESL readers include *My Side of the Mountain* (178 pages), about teenager Sam who carves out a home in the trunk of a tree in upstate New York, and *There's an Owl in the Shower* (133 pages), about Borden who comes to value the endangered short-eared owl, despite his father's loss of his job as a logger. George's language is often complex and at times a bit lofty; her longer works are most accessible to advanced readers. However, the books mentioned contain such fast action and memorable characters that students at the intermediate level can enjoy hearing them read aloud, especially when supported by exercises like those described in chapter 2.

3. Physics and Chemistry

Michael Dahl's *Inclined Planes* introduces a principle of mechanics. With few words and many illustrations the author demonstrates the definition and uses of inclined planes for beginning learners of English. Directions for a simple science experiment make hands-on learning easy. Other similar books in the series teach about levers, pulleys, and wheels and axles.

Walter Wick's *Optical Tricks* contains thirteen illusions based on tricks of illustration in fourteen pages of simple, direct text. Suitable for both teens and adults as well as middle schoolers, this breezy discussion about the relationships of shapes and angles could be read aloud to high-beginner-level speakers and read silently by intermediate students. *A Drop of Water* by the same author explains the properties of water with simple, direct text illustrated with amazingly clear photographs by this talented artist. This is suitable for readers from middle school age and up with low-intermediate reading skills.

4. General

Who could ignore Joanna Cole's Magic School Bus series illustrated with much comic relief by Bruce Deger? In *The Human Body,* the inimitable Ms. Frizzle takes her class through the body of the unsuspecting Arnold, a classmate who made the mistake of eating junk food and daydreaming. The text is intermediate level because of the many conversational asides, snide remarks, and puns, but the illustrations are fairly specific, and many young students will be highly motivated to struggle beyond what is easy for them. The information is sound and complete. These are books that will keep readers' attention for hours, noting all the jokes embedded in the illustrations and text. Ms. Frizzle's students are wonderfully suspicious of their teacher and sardonic to each other. It captures the culture of middle school classrooms perfectly. However, adults and older teens may balk at the silliness.

Margaret Spense's *Fossil Fuel* is part of an educational series, The World Around Us, in which each book of about thirty pages describes important controversial subjects like acid rain, nuclear waste, solar power, the ozone layer, tropical rain forests, and other topics relevant to environmental issues. The short introduction is followed by an illustrated overview spread over two pages, which serves as a cognitive map of the subject. Each concept is illustrated with colorful sketches, and each piece of text is fairly short. However, each page is so dense with new information that it would be best to teach most language learners only a double-spread page during each lesson. The glossary and index could provide practice in locating subjects and reading definitions. This series should appeal to adolescents and adults who may lack advanced language skills but need sophisticated information.

EXERCISES FOR BASIC BOOKS ABOUT SCIENCE

1. To provide practice in writing and relevant vocabulary, rewrite very basic children's books like Eric Carle's *The Very Hungry Caterpillar,* using other animals (the very busy ant . . . the very proud lion . . . the very timid bird).

2. As part of a group or class project, ask intermediate-level students to write and illustrate a similar series of science books. Provide a format or list of topics to be covered so the books will be somewhat predictable for beginning-level students. For example, a series about minerals could include a physical description, chemical makeup, the geographic sources, and common uses. Even young children can follow similar outlines using illustrated encyclopedias or series books. Some may even try to write stories about a magic school bus or a magic skateboard—which would be easy to draw.

Most important in teaching math and science concepts is not the specific materials or books used, but the attitude of the teacher about these content areas. In Western culture, math and science have had the reputation of being difficult to learn, especially for people from non-academic or nonscholarly backgrounds. Often the special terms and language that mathematicians and scientists use to explain their subjects seem like so much magical verse, used to maintain their special expertise and authority. Books, teachers, pictures, and other educational resources that present these same concepts in more familiar terms and metaphors are good introductions; once students know the concepts, the "special" language is easier to adopt.

Teachers of new English-language learners need to make an extra effort to wave away the magic smoke of academic jargon and to raise the confidence of their students so they too can participate as practitioners of math and science. There is no special talent needed, only a willingness to find the connections between familiar words and the Latinate terms used by experts. Hispanic students can find similar root words in their native vocabularies; asking them to help their English-speaking peers may highlight this advantage and raise confidence in their linguistic ability to participate in schooling.

CHAPTER 7

Focus on Multicultural Themes

MULTICULTURAL LITERATURE provides information about the various ethnic and cultural roots of the North American population. More important for new learners of American English, it also models current culturally acceptable ways of reacting to differences. Almost all literature published by major companies in the United States for young people in the last twenty years teaches, preaches, and exemplifies the multicultural ethic of respecting and even welcoming individuals with innate differences, whether they are physical, ethnic, or mental. Many books for young people also encourage toleration and respect for cultural differences, including those based on various beliefs about gender, religion, and family configurations.

While many American teachers take these ideals for granted, students new to this culture may have inherited other ideas from their families and from their experiences in a different social culture. Multicultural literature can infuse language teaching with the ideals of respect for diversity that are part of our public school tradition. Whether or not new students accept these ideals, we have offered them the opportunity to learn the acceptable manners and language for entering into the American mainstream. I voice this optimism with deep awareness of the often reprehensible treatment of different peoples that has occurred in our nation.

While I have sometimes been inwardly jolted by ideas or expressions from new students from other cultures, I am also often aware that some of my language and manners can seem coarse or inappropriate for a woman "of a certain age" in their eyes. Gentle guidance is more helpful in these cases than blame or shame. Multicultural literature provides a useful context to discover and discuss these cultural differences at an impersonal distance.

In the history of the United States, the land and the freedoms promised by its government have never been severely threatened by people of other ethnic groups, people designated as "the enemy." Thus it is sometimes difficult for us to understand the depth of cultural antipathies of some people toward others. "Political correctness" demands that we avoid labels that designate separateness from the mainstream or, more accurately, avoid any sense of historical strife or blame; the current ethic of American public education demands an obliteration of all past hatreds or battles. Can we, in the United States—where most of us have the luxury of not worrying about unwarranted searches of our homes or arrests without due cause or the overnight devaluation of our money and all of our goods—can we assume the right to ask immigrants from other cultures (sometimes unwilling immigrants) to forget their personal histories? Again, we need to be gentle and tolerant of prejudices that we may not thoroughly comprehend.

Fortunately there are many books that exemplify, rather than preach and patronize, the ideals of equal rights and respect for people of all genders, ethnicities, and ages in a format and style appropriate for new English learners. Included here is just a minuscule sample of the excellent books available. Each represents a slightly different treatment of the multicultural ethic.

A RANGE OF BOOK TYPES: AFRICAN AMERICANS

Most newcomers to the United States have heard about the historical plight of African Americans. Some immigrants have exaggerated notions of interracial violence or segregation. Multicultural literature focusing on the African American experience allows new language learners to ask relevant questions.

A good beginning is Ezra Jack Keats's *The Snowy Day*. This Caldecott Award picture book never mentions race or even depicts anything remotely multicultural; it is a book about a young boy playing in the snow, too young to join a snowball fight, but old enough to go out again the next day with a friend. The text is fairly simple and would be appropriate for a beginner, a perfect book to introduce when snow is expected. The little boy happens to be African American, only obvious because the distinctive shade of his skin is highlighted when encased in a bright red snow suit and when he rises above the tub when taking a bath. The book is remarkable because it is so unselfconscious in regards to race. Peter's first identity is as an adventurous young boy, who revels in the pleasures of snow. His second identity is as a child who takes refuge in the safety of a home where his cold clothes are removed and a bath warms his body. Only incidentally is Peter "African American." For new arrivals to the country, this implicit attitude can speak more forcefully than words about one ideal of multiculturalism, where differences are merely interesting, and what a child dreams and does is more worthy of comment than the shade of his skin.

 Exercises:

    1. Ask about the readers' experiences with snow. "Have you seen snow piled up high in the street? Have you walked on snow and heard it crunch? Have you pretended you were a mountain climber? What have you done that Peter did?" These questions should point out similarities (or differences) that pertain more to experience than racial identity.

    2. Depending on your geography, help new students draw, tell, and write about a day "in the city" or "in the mountains" or "in the heat," using native-language speakers as resources.

Donald Crew's *Big Mama* is a reminiscence of the train ride down to Grandmother's house in the rural South of the 1940s. Again, no overt mention is made of racism or multicultural issues, but the train car has a sign designating it as "colored," and no representatives of other racial groups are included. This portrait of life in a segregated America is full of family warmth and joy despite the restrictions imposed by an invisible majority; it depicts a sliver of African American history as lived by "ordinary" people who have the spirit to celebrate who they are and where they come from.

Robert Coles's *The Story of Ruby Bridges* is a retelling of a historical event, the integration of an elementary school in the 1960s. It portrays the struggle toward a national acceptance of multiculturalism, and the courage of one participant. The language is simple, appropriate for low-intermediate or even beginning learners with read-aloud support, but the tone and the message are profound. A young girl persists in attending school, insisting on an education despite the resistance of her more powerful peers and adults. A recent autobiography by Ruby Bridges, *Through My Eyes*, is a useful accompaniment, with many photos that make Robert Coles's story terrifyingly real as well as placing her story in a wider historical context. The accompanying text is simple to understand, though the length (fifty-nine pages) is more suitable for intermediate-level readers.

🚲 *Exercises:*

1. Help your students identify aspects of African American culture (or another culture) that celebrate life, or that add positively to global culture. What has the United States gained from African American culture?

2. Ask students to imagine acts of courage that someone might accomplish that might advance equal opportunity for all?

3. Ask your students to relate (aloud or in writing) stories from their own experiences that advance social justice.

A historical overview of the African American experience, clearly written with helpful illustrations, is Walter Dean Myers's *Now Is Your Time: The African-American Struggle for Freedom*. The author uses his personal family story over generations to provide a continuous thread that adds interest to this history. Supported by pictures and photos of authentic documents, this would be appropriate for intermediate and advanced language learners. Reading this thoughtful perspective will not only reinforce the American history taught in most textbooks, but trace its major events from the viewpoint of African Americans, an immigrant group brought here without regard to their will. Most recent immigrants to the United States will find parallels to their own histories.

🚲 *Exercises*:

1. Help each of your students begin to construct a family history centered on their own entry into the United States, and related to the emigration patterns of their countries of origin. Be sensitive to students who may be reluctant to share family information for safety reasons or because of a sense of personal privacy. Offer the option of interviewing an older friend or relative, or suggest that they tell the story of a fictionalized character from their own culture. Incorporate family histories into a class booklet. Questions might include:

    a. How far back can we trace our family on any side?
    b. Where are the places we have lived?
    c. What kinds of work has our family done?
    d. What traditional meals does our family eat?
    e. How do we celebrate holidays?

2. Help your students participate with other classmates to make a time line that traces their family, personal, or ethnic histories in a format that highlights parallels to U.S. history.

Harlem: A Poem by Walter Dean Myers and his son, Christopher Myers, celebrates with vivid colors and simple language the spirit and rhythms of that well-known section of New York City. While not for the literal-minded learner who worries about the definition of each expression or word, this book would be fun for learners who like to play with sounds.

🚲 *Exercises:*

1. Encourage students to paint pictures and dictate text that mimics the sounds of their own neighborhoods or favorite

places. Collect samples for a class bulletin board. Since using paint is a special treat for many students, and new language learners are no exception, this exercise may motivate them to compose text with more expressive language. Use volunteers who are willing listeners to help students explore language possibilities to find the most appropriate vocabulary and phrases.

2. Begin collecting names of famous people who lived in Harlem throughout its history and post a list on a bulletin board or web page. Keep parallel lists of well-known people from your home locale and from the areas where your students have lived. Include not just celebrities, but community figures who generate interest, gossip, or admiration for the ways they live their lives. This project, which may stretch from a few weeks to most of the year, helps students become aware of the varied types of people who contribute to the world's well-being, and it fosters considerable pride. This list may encourage students to be more aware of the news media.

SPARKING CONTROVERSY TO ENCOURAGE LANGUAGE SKILLS

Alice Walker's *To Hell with Dying* has only twenty-four pages of easily read text, but its themes are most suitable for mature teen and adult intermediate readers. This autobiographical reminiscence by Alice Walker lovingly focuses on her childhood memories of reviving Mr. Sweet from his near-death illnesses merely by being children who pay attention to their neighbor. In accessible ordinary language with wonderful detail, Walker demonstrates that a person does not have to be perfect to be loved. This story is a good source for discussing the effects of poverty and racism, and for instilling the wisdom of accepting life's disappointments without bitterness. It is an accurate portrayal of people not often met and loved in literature, in particular a neighbor who drinks alcohol to blunt his disappointment in life, yet who is a loving friend to the children.

Although this book may be easy to dismiss as potentially controversial, it can arouse a strong desire in students to make their opinions understood by others. Using this book with more than one language learner usually encourages more discussion, as students seem to take courage from each other; they are inspired to stretch beyond the edge of their present language capabilities to share their opinions. Students with fewer language skills listen hard, struggling to understand their more advanced peers. After new language learners read and discuss this story, try using it, or a similar book involving controversial topics, in a larger group including native speakers. Letting new language learners read the book in a cooperative fashion, as described in the third chapter, and practice the relevant language and skills will provide them a chance to participate more fully in the whole group discussion.

Multicultural issues as presented in books for young people are good topics to help students practice the skills of critical thinking, logical argument, and effective oral expression because these issues affect everyone. Of course it is important to remember that students from some cultures may find it distasteful or unnatural to enter into discussions where they are asked to express individual opinions, especially if they are different from others. Disagreement is considered rude in some cultures. Modeling polite discussions can encourage these students to become more assertive yet retain their traditional sense of communal cohesiveness, a skill they may need in order to succeed in American academic settings.

LEARNING ABOUT OTHER CULTURES

In the United States, most new learners of English entering public schools are from a Latino culture. Many new books as well as beloved classics of children's literature are now translated into Spanish; a resource for those books is included in the bibliography. Many other books describe experiences of Latino immigrants and descendants in the United States. Some intersperse Spanish vocabulary and expressions into the text, which reinforces the reading skills of beginning learners of English. *Mama Provi and the Pot of Rice* by Sylvia Rosa-Casanova tells a story of a grandmother from Puerto Rico who loves to cook for large numbers of people. When her granddaughter Lucy becomes ill with chicken pox and can't make her daily visit, Mama Provi cooks up a large pot of arroz con pollo to take to her. As she makes the long climb up to Lucy's apartment on the eighth floor, Mama Provi trades bowls of her chicken and rice for some bread, black beans, collards, tea, and apple pie. This modernized version of the stone soup theme in which everyone donates a bit of food to concoct a fabulous meal contains a few Spanish phrases within the simple English text. The frequent repetitions make this a book suitable for younger readers with beginning or low-intermediate skills. Another beginning-level text is Tony Johnston's *The Iguana Brothers: Presenting a Tale of Two Lizards*. This tongue-in-cheek story of two iguanas also contains a few Spanish words inserted into the short English text, both languages easily understood in context. The iguanas take siestas, watch the stars and enjoy life. The humor is lazy and dry but most likely attractive to middle school types.

Exercises:

1. After reading it with students who will probably enjoy the humor, ask if this book portrays stereotypes of Latino culture. If so, is it a good book to read in a classroom? What would make the book more suitable?

2. If your students are not Spanish-speaking, do they enjoy learning a few words from yet another language? What are the advantages of learning new languages? Are there disadvantages to learning more than one language at the same time?

Gary Soto's *Snapshots for the Wedding* describes a Mexican American wedding in the voice of the flower girl Mayan. Illustrated with humor and pizzazz by Stephanie Garcia's clay figures and found objects, this simple text would be more suitable for intermediate readers than for beginning learners; the metaphors are complex and not clearly illustrated. One of the most prominent Latino writers of fiction for young people, Gary Soto describes the lives of Mexican Americans in California with striking metaphors and imagery. His precise portrayals of complex characters and exact descriptions make his literature accessible to highly motivated intermediate readers or students with advanced skills. The dramatic story of Eddie, a college student who is inextricably pulled into the violence of his urban neighborhood in Soto's novel *Buried Onions* would engage intermediate and advanced readers to stretch their English-language reading skills. A glossary of Spanish words assists readers who do not read Spanish. Soto's collection of short stories, *Baseball in April and Other Stories*, could be used with intermediate and advanced readers as a text for reading aloud.

Two annual awards for Latino literature for young readers are good resources for selecting worthy texts. One is the Pura Belpré Award by the American Library Association for Latino/Latina writers and illustrators. Another major prize is the Americas Award, begun in 1993. Sponsored by the National Consortium of Latin American Studies Programs (CLASP), it honors authentic representations of Latin American and Hispanic life experiences. Both organizations also publish lists of recommended books.

BIOGRAPHIES

Most biographies are difficult for new language learners unless there is a particular motivation to know about the subject, and this is true of multicultural biographies as well. Visual aids such as time lines and pictures, as well as supporting material from the Internet, reference books, and illustrated histories, are fairly easy to find.

Allen Say's *Grandfather's Journey* tells the story of a Japanese man who immigrates to the United States, then returns to Japan. He misses California while in Japan, and misses Japan while in California. The respectful tone and lovely pictures celebrate both cultures.

Also accessible and useful for depicting how people manage to bridge cultures is the autobiography of Maria Tallchief, written with Rosemary Wells and illustrated by Gary Kelley, *Tallchief: America's Prima Ballerina*. Written when Tallchief was seventy-five years old, the style is straightforward and plain but salted with the wonderful details that can enhance history as focused on one person's life. Tallchief tells the story of her childhood on the Osage Indian reservation after oil was discovered, making the Osage nation very rich; her father drove a long red Pierce Arrow. The traditional way of life was illegal in the United States, but Tallchief (born Elizabeth Marie and called Betty as a girl) heard the drumming and saw the dancing anyway. Her Scots-Irish mother introduced her to music. When she was young, the family moved to Los Angeles, where eventually Maria studied with the famous Russian ballet master Nijinsky. At seventeen, she went to New York City to join the Ballet Russe de Monte Carlo. Beautifully told with no distance or false delicacy, this is a story of a happy woman who lives with music inside her. This story is a great antidote to the notion of Native Americans as quaint, dirty, or drunken victims of European domination. It is a story that incorporates both dimensions, celebrating what can be achieved despite the prejudices and injustices visited on cultural minorities in the United States. The twenty-eight pages are illustrated with richly colored pastels with the slight mistiness of memories. The language is suitable for low-intermediate readers, but the interest level is appropriate for all ages.

Native American culture fascinates many young people, especially those who have lived in other countries. *Who Were the First North Americans?* by Philippa Wingate and Steven Reid provides a short conversational overview with detailed, colorful illustrations. John Clare's *North American Indian Life* is only thirty pages long, but stuffed with interesting facts about the lifestyles, food, technology, and accomplishments of Indians from every region of the United States. Brightly illustrated with photographs and drawings, this encyclopedic text does not include modern-day Native American life.

If You Lived with the Hopi by Anne Kamma does include both traditional and modern life in its eighty-page discussion, posing questions like "What would happen if you were bad?" and answering in about four paragraphs of text. *If You Lived with the Sioux* by Ann McGovern uses the same format to portray another group. Large print, simple language, imaginative questions, and maps showing where in the United States these groups live make this series an interesting text for low-intermediate readers of all ages.

MODELING THE MEETING OF CULTURES

Some literature depicts the challenge of fitting into a new cultural environment. Many picture books demonstrate how students who feel different find that others accept them when they make the effort to communicate what they can do.

Baseball Saved Us by Ken Mochizuki, with pastel drawings by Dom Lee, is a simply written story of the long, discouraging days during the World War II internment of people of Japanese descent. The boredom, the fear, the resentment, and the isolation of a prison camp causes restlessness and unease. When a baseball team is organized, the children begin to thrive. Finally one boy, particularly small for his age, wins the grudging respect of, first, his peers in the prison camp and then, when he returns to school after the war, even his non-Japanese classmates. The short paragraphs of simple direct text are sensitively written with a comfortable happy ending. Older readers with low proficiency as well as younger children could enjoy this book.

Another example of this theme is Linda Crew's *Children of the River* about a young teenage girl from Vietnam who tries to bridge the distance between her parents' traditional family values and those of an American high school, where the blond blue-eyed football star seems fated to date a conventionally pretty cheerleader. In this young adult novel, suitable for reading aloud to intermediate-level preteens, the football star shows more depth than the stereotype; the ending is a bit too wonderful to believe, but the book does model open-minded behaviors.

Other literature describes environments in which all kinds of cultural differences are welcomed and the strengths from each are emphasized to the benefit of all. One such book is Steve Schuch's *A Symphony of Whales*. The fourteen pages of text describe an actual event that begins with the girl Glashka who hears music in her head; the old ones of her people tell her that she hears the songs of the ancient whale Narna. When Glashka takes the reins of her family's sled dogs on the way back from a trip, they run toward the ocean, where hundreds of whales are trapped in the bay by the ice. Glashka's mother calls a Russian icebreaker to come and free them. After trying several kinds of music, beginning with whale's songs, to no avail, the ship finally broadcasts a recording of classical music. The music of Beethoven attracts the whales who respond and follow the boat out to safety. Told in a straightforward, sensible fashion, this story describes Inuit life in Alaska without any sense of quaintness or paternalism. The painted illustrations capture the heavy gray mist and wetness of deep winter. There are no igloos or Eskimo folk feel; this book depicts a thoroughly modern society but one that retains a connection with its traditional legends.

R. Friedman takes a look at modern multiculturalism in *How My Parents Learned to Eat*. In this short book of thirty-two pages, an American sailor and a Japanese girl practice eating, one with a fork and spoon, and the other with chopsticks. Now married, they alternate implements, depending on the type of meal they are eating.

Allen Say's *Tree of Cranes* with fifteen pages of text and fourteen illustrated pages is accessible to low intermediate students because of the simple language and short sentence patterns. This story told by a young Japanese boy describes a Christmas day in Japan, when his mother, remembering her former life in California, decorates a tree with origami cranes. A meeting of two cultures is beautifully portrayed by this author/illustrator who uses this theme often in his books.

Intermediate readers may enjoy the series by Lensey Namioka about the Chinese family of the Yangs whose life in America is full of amusing contradictions. One advantage of these light-hearted novels is that multiculturalism is not the only focus; the Yang children have fully developed personalities independent of their heritage, and their stories could happen in any modern middle-class family. *Yang the Third and Her Impossible Family* describes her brother—more fully portrayed in *Yang the Youngest and His Terrible Ear*—and sister, who all appear in *Yang the Second and Her Secret Admirers.*

America Street: A Multicultural Anthology of Stories edited by Anne Mazer collects fourteen short stories of about nine pages each that describe the meeting of cultures in the United States. They range from light-hearted to wistful, and include tales about modern Native American, Asian, African American, and Arab American characters. Because of the use of dialect and the lack of illustrations, this book is more suitable for readers and listeners of intermediate and advanced proficiency.

RESOURCES FOR FINDING MULTICULTURAL LITERATURE

Most publishers label multicultural literature in their catalogs and web sites; some libraries separate multicultural literature, but others consider the term so broad and difficult to define that they use it more as an adjective for specific genres like poetry, novels, and picture books. Since Americans increasingly participate in a variety of cultural settings, the term multicultural becomes increasingly inclusive. One text that is helpful in delineating books for young people is Donna Norton's *Multicultural Children's Literature: Through the Eyes of Many Children*. Literature by and about African American, Native American, Latino, Asian, Jewish, and Middle Eastern representatives is described and discussed in helpful detail. A time line for each category highlights the oral and literary traditions as they pertain to literature for children. The author raises and attempts to answer relevant questions for each culture. Each section contains extensive annotated bibliographies.

International literature for people in the United States is defined as literature originally published in other countries, but not necessarily in another language. An annotated bibliography of over seven hundred volumes, Carl Tomlinson's *Children's Books from Other Countries*, is useful for classroom teachers as it differentiates between realistic texts, fantasy tales, and informational picture books for the very young, and these same kinds of books for older children, as well as surveying poetry, biography, and anthologies. Most of the books are from Great Britain, Australia, Canada, Switzerland, Sweden, and Japan, but a few are from other nations too. The commentary about international literature is comprehensive and expert.

Just because a book is international or multicultural doesn't mean that it is useful for second-language learners. Many times authors attempt to capture the language patterns of a particular culture in a way that adds panache, but may add an extra obstacle to a reader who is still struggling to understand the basic meanings and patterns of standard English. Translations often result in English with a different rhythm or vocabulary. Pictures and print don't always match in a helpful way. However, as the world knits itself into a tighter ball, educating young people will inevitably focus more frequently and profoundly on multicultural issues. Students who are learning English as a second (or third) language can provide a valuable perspective to their peers who speak only English and who have experienced only the homogenized view of American television.

CHAPTER 8

When Most Students Don't Speak English

STATISTICS FROM THE National Clearinghouse for Bilingual Education (NCBE) in 1999 indicate that half of all teachers will educate a new English-language learner during their careers. In many areas of the country, this percentage is closer to 90 percent. A U.S. Census Brief released in August 2000 indicates that about one-tenth of the U.S. population (about 25.8 million) is foreign-born, the highest percentage since 1930. Studies by the National Center for Education Statistics indicate that only a third of teachers with English-language learners in their classrooms have had any professional development in teaching these students. Nationally, teachers are receiving mixed messages about the best way to teach students whose dominant language is not English, especially when they make up the majority or even a large percentage of students in the classroom.

This chapter begins with a historical overview of bilingual education in the United States because in my own learning I found it helpful to understand the various definitions and opinions surrounding this controversial issue to figure out how best to plan my teaching. Teaching a class in which the majority of students are not native English speakers is a wonderful opportunity because they are all more expert than I in certain aspects, and I could count on that expertise in planning lessons. However, I certainly didn't want that sharing of their diverse expertise to get in the way of their progress in learning English. The ongoing discussion about the merits and challenges of bilingual education raises many questions for teachers to solve using the data gathered from their unique population and situations.

A BRIEF OVERVIEW OF BILINGUAL EDUCATION IN THE UNITED STATES

Before the beginning of the twentieth century, bilingual education, or education in a language other than English, was not abnormal. In Wisconsin and other nearby states, a number of public schools taught in German, Norwegian, Dutch, and Swedish. In New Mexico, an 1884 law established schools in which literacy was to be achieved in either Spanish or English. Beginning with the large waves of immigration and the acquisition of new territory by the United States in the last half of the nineteenth century, educators and politicians expressed fears that the "onslaught" of new cultures would overwhelm the traditional customs and language of this nation, still relatively new by European and Asian standards and only recently re-united after the Civil War. The unifying effect of the two world wars, drawing diverse ethnic groups together in a common cause, and the rise of the United States as a world leader in wealth jelled that determination to define "American" as a distinct culture. Public education for everyone became an important goal during the first half of the twentieth century. The purpose was to immerse all students in an educational melting pot; the aim was to smooth out differences and to create homogenized American citizens with middle-class values and aspirations. The Civil Rights movements of the sixties questioned this agenda. Most pertinent to this discussion were the Chicano and Latino voices that questioned the impact of English-only education on Spanish-speaking children. The first bilingual programs of the 1970s provided instruction in Spanish in kindergarten and the primary grades for Spanish-speaking children, helping them develop skills and build up a content-specific knowledge base, while they were hearing English sounds, words, and sentence structures from language instruction, from their environment in non-academic subjects such as music and physical education, and from the general school environment. Beginning in the middle grades, English- and Spanish-speaking students were increasingly integrated and taught in both languages. By that time Spanish-speaking children had already learned the skills necessary for reading, computation, and the kinds of learning that happen in schools at the same rate as their English-speaking peers. Both were able to focus on learning those basic skills in their dominant language without the frustrating obstacles of concurrently struggling with a foreign language. The goal of this educational model is to provide bilingual and bicultural education to all children. This type of program was the intent of most educators who supported early political efforts to develop more bilingual programs.

The Bilingual Education Act of 1968 (BEA) began as Title VII of the Elementary and Secondary Education Act of 1965. It provided funds to educational programs to develop instructional materials for low-income non-English-speaking students, to recruit and train personnel for bilingual programs, and to establish and maintain programs for teaching English as a second language. In the first few years these programs and their personnel were assumed to be bilingual, as described above, with teachers who could and did teach in two languages. However, some schools found it difficult to participate. Sparked by legal battles about responsibilities of school districts to provide ESL instruction, the Office of Civil Rights issued a memorandum in 1970 that stated that the civil rights of non-English-speaking students were being treated differently if the curriculum was in English because they were not receiving an equal education.

While this served as a wake-up call to schools, that they could not ignore or discriminate against a student with limited English proficiency, the law did not specify that bilingual education in the student's dominant language was the solution. Many schools developed "subtractive" programs that offered extra English instruction to immigrant children but did not offer instruction in their own language. Further laws and bills sought to change this situation, which was addressed most effectively in the 1988 amendment to the Bilingual Education Act which stipulated that 75 percent of any federal money received by schools be allocated to transitional bilingual educational programs. With some exceptions, students were limited to a period of up to three years in these environments before they would be fully integrated into regular classrooms. Furthermore, the criteria for moving from bilingual instruction into all-English programs were to be explained to the parents in their dominant language. The remaining quarter of the federal monies could be spent on special alternative instruction.

In the 1989 case, *Teresa v. Berkeley Unified School District*, the court found that ESL and bilingual teachers did not need special credentials to implement either of these programs. The court also failed to differentiate between monolingual teachers of English as a second language and bilingual teachers, so schools can offer English instruction by a teacher who has no knowledge of her students' dominant language. The 1990s brought a sharp increase in politically active groups supporting English-only in government and in schools. By 1998, only twenty-two states allowed schools to use any language other than English for instruction. In 1996, the Republican presidential candidates officially opposed bilingual instruction to garner political support. During the years of the Clinton administration, funds increased to the Office of Bilingual Education and Minority Language Affairs of the Department of Education. While bilingual education is considered too impractical to mandate, in part because the current overall shortage of teachers pales next to the shortage of bilingual teachers, public policy makers seem to be recognizing the importance of respecting different cultures and languages and encouraging Americans of every ethnic group to increase their knowledge of languages other than English.

The immediate future for bilingual education seems dim. Experts in language education recognize that helping students learn content and reading skills in the dominant language is theoretically more efficient, because information and ideas transfer easily into other languages. However, the reality is that many ESL students fail to make a transition to competency in academic or professional level

English-language skills. The situation is complicated where many do not speak the same dominant language. While they learn enough English for basic interpersonal communication, many ESL students avoid moving beyond their comfort level, remaining in community situations in which their first language is dominant. This tendency perpetuates the exclusion of language communities from the mainstream where academic and professional English is necessary. Many bilingual programs are being abandoned, even outside the United States, because the participants have failed to show academic or professional success at increased rates when compared with the success rate of immersion programs. Since 1998, many students in California who were switched out of bilingual programs into English immersion education have shown a significant increase in their standardized test scores. Creating a classroom community that encourages everyone to participate to the best of his or her abilities will increase the chances that everyone strives to learn English as a way to communicate with the largest number of people.

CREATING COMMUNITY IN A MULTILINGUAL CLASSROOM

One expert in bilingual and multilingual teaching, Christian Faltis, lists five conditions that should exist to "promote two-way communication and social integration within the linguistically diverse English-medium classroom" (p. 1). Paraphrased and simplified, they are:

1. All members of the classroom community should be communicating with each other with equal frequency;
2. All students should interact socially with each other;
3. All lessons should be planned to include second-language acquisition instruction along with the content;
4. All members of the local community should be equally encouraged to participate in the activities related to school;
5. All school activities should foster equal rights and opportunities for all members of the community (pp. 1–2).

Experienced teachers realize that these conditions are a hundred times easier to list than to accomplish every day in every classroom. Fortunately, literature for children and young adults can help focus attention on cooperative communication rather than divisive competition. As soon as possible, help students from both or all language groups feel welcome.

a. Ask students to write a few sentences in their dominant language:

"Hello, my name is _____." "Good!" "Good-bye." "Thank you."

If the students are unwilling or unable to participate, ask for help from other sources. Also try to learn how to pronounce these phrases, as well as your students' names. Help everyone in your class practice the correct pronunciation, and correct (politely) any mispronounced names you hear, especially from the front office. It is vitally important to indicate that an authority representing the school values each student's first or dominant language, even if it is not English. Even if students or parents seem to want to downplay their native culture in order to become "American," showing interest in and appreciation for each language will send a message that your school supports a multicultural ethic, outlined above.

b. Include books about each culture in your classroom library as much as possible, or keep a supply checked out from your school library. Some resources for finding out about good books representing different cultures are mentioned in chapter 7 and in the bibliography.

c. Include a few books, magazines, or other items in each student's original language. Demonstrate that learning even a few words or phrases from several languages is not impossible; it may take frequent practice over a period of days and regular use of these phrases over a period of weeks and months. Try to include a few brief practice drills for words or phrases in the languages of your students in your weekly routine. Many language instructors believe that the more people know about different languages, the more aware they become of the grammar, structure, and vocabulary of their own language. Certainly, helping students become aware of different languages may help them become better readers and writers about multicultural issues.

d. If you do not know the dominant language of some of your students, encourage them to teach a few phrases to you and the others in your class. This is when the phrase "a community of learners" is really possible, because the students become the real experts. Ask students to translate for each other when it seems helpful.

In learning the language skills of listening, reading, writing, and even speaking, cooperative learning is effective and efficient. There is little point in asking someone to use a dictionary when the main focus of the lesson is comprehension of information or an idea. Knowing how to use a dictionary is useful, but it is easier and more natural to get a translation from a fellow student. However, make sure that the same students don't always speak for others who may be more quiet, and establish the routine of asking your students to repeat the new English word or phrase two or three times, so they won't need to ask for translation in the future. Periodically, ask your native English speakers to repeat words or phrases from the other languages, especially when they apply to important or relevant information.

e. In classes where only one or two other languages than English are spoken, try to find translations of the same book, preferably a short, easy-to-read book that is attractive to most of your students. Take turns reading, asking a student to read the first page in his or her dominant language. Then ask all students to shadow read, following the leader, sentence by sentence. Read about a fourth of the book this way, depending on its length. Then switch to another language. If the dominant classroom language is English, begin with the text in another language.

Ask each student to summarize as much as they understand about the plot, characters, and setting, and then compare notes. Then let students work cooperatively as a class to correct any misconceptions or to fill in any blanks. Finally, provide students with a photocopy of the text in a language other than their dominant language and ask them to write a free translation. Asking for a written translation will encourage attention to details. If some of the text is written in a non-Roman alphabet, ask native speakers to explain (as much as possible) the significance of one or two symbols. After a period of individual work, allow students to complete their translations in pairs or small groups of similar language. This exercise will teach all participants quite a bit about language learning, and make them more conscious of the challenges facing their peers. This will also serve as a community-building exercise as various students become the experts in their language and leaders of the class. Encourage pride among classmates in multilingualism, and publicize the linguistic accomplishments of your class.

CLASSROOMS IN WHICH SPANISH AND ENGLISH DOMINATE

The U.S. Census brief mentioned at the beginning of the chapter reported that about half of the foreign-born population in the United States or 5 percent of the U.S. population comes from Latin America and speaks Spanish as their dominant language. To introduce Spanish to English classmates, and to show respect for Latino culture and the Spanish language in the classroom, read aloud, or ask students to read aloud books in English that feature Spanish words. One such attractive book for beginning readers is Arthur Dorros's *Abuela*, the story of a young boy and his elderly aunt in New York City. The English text is interspersed with Spanish vocabulary, and a Spanish-to-English glossary helps new learners of English read definitions. Spanish-speaking students may be motivated to read aloud, since the Spanish words are familiar. For young and older readers, a book by the same author describes a tradition common in most South American countries, the celebration of Carnival. The thirty-two pages of *Por fin es carnaval (Tonight Is Carnaval)* are illustrated by pictures of South American fabric art photographed by members of the Club de Madres Virgen del Carmen of Lima, Peru. The cheerful story outlines the preparations for the Carnival of a family in a village of the Andes.

Another short text, suitable for introducing Spanish to a classroom in which it is unfamiliar is Verna Aardema's *Borreguita and the Coyote*. This is sectioned into folktales told in serial fashion about a lamb that tricks a coyote out of eating her. The coyote's refrain, is woven into "Está bien," the dialogue, which is mostly English. The slightly sardonic tone is tongue-in-cheek and fun to read. One way to present this to a class would be to ask Spanish-dominant students to practice reading it in English until they feel proficient, and then read it aloud to their English-dominant peers, leading them in a choral chant of "Está bien." A short book by a well-known children's author that contains its own translation is Pat Mora's *Listen to the Desert/Oye al desierto*. This slim picture book tells about the sounds different creatures make on the desert.

For more mature readers of Spanish and English at a beginning level, Jonah Winter's *Diego*, strikingly illustrated by Jeanette Winter and translated by Amy Prince, is a relatively short book of forty pages with pictures to support the text. This biography of the Mexican artist Diego Rivera, who is most famous for his murals depicting the lives and struggles of the poor, is a good way to instill pride in Mexican culture. It would be a good choice for using both the English and Spanish versions to practice reading skills in both languages.

For mature readers, Gary Paulsen's *Sisters/Hermanas*, translated by Gloria de Aragon Andujar, is a brief bleak story juxtaposing the life of Traci, driven by her competitive mother to win a spot on the cheerleading team, and Rosa, a fourteen-year-old illegal Mexican immigrant who survives life in Texas by selling her body. The two meet for a single moment in a mall. The subject matter is controversial, but that might be an advantage in motivating discussion by girls angry at the stereotypes portrayed in this book. The simple power of these sixty-six pages of prose is a strong incentive to read, and the English and Spanish versions placed side by side are helpful for learners of both languages. One way to handle this novel is to ask students to read aloud the language they are learning, and check the translation only afterward. For students who are below intermediate level, reading the translation silently after reading each page aloud may develop fluency by maintaining comprehension and interest in the story. Students should also try to participate in discussions in the language they are learning, even if they must ask for help in their native language before they repeat what they want to say in their new language. Conversations in both English and Spanish are helpful to all participants trying to learn about language, as each strives to follow the thread of authentic speech. Learning some Spanish words and constructions will help native English speakers become more conscious of the Latinate vocabulary roots and the grammatical structure of their own language. Learning another language enables students to compare their own language as a socially constructed artifact, dependent more on each individual's environment than on native intelligence.

Extremely useful for any institution serving a bilingual Spanish-English population is Isabel Schon's *Recommended Books in Spanish for Children and Young Adults, 1991–1995* and *1996–1999*. This annotated list of books for children and adolescents includes reference books and other nonfiction covering a wide range of topics from religion, cookery, and folklore, to science, technology, history, arts and crafts, and publishers' series. Fiction is divided into easy reading and general-level fiction. Many are translations of books first published in English. Books are indexed by author, title, and subject. The commentary not only summarizes the contents of each text but also describes its visual and stylistic qualities as well as the qualities of the translation. Recent visits to the bookstore indicate that an increasing number of books for children and young adults, from Dr. Seuss books to Harry Potter, are available in Spanish translations. These are helpful in encouraging new learners of English to expand their reading, checking their comprehension by themselves.

Jane Feder's short tale, *Table, Chair, Bear: A Book in Many Languages,* is a model of the kind of multilingual education that would be ideal for our increasingly global community. Listing the names of several items in four languages, this book lets young readers become aware that other languages exist, and lets them practice their sounds. We should all know common words and phrases in many languages, and become as language-rich as possible. Using texts of many languages in classrooms begins the process by demonstrating a respect for languages other than English, as well as a deeper understanding of those aspects of English which reflect its many roots. While learning about another language doesn't guarantee mutual understanding or even tolerance, it does open a window for at least minimal communication, and makes other people seem less frightening and foreign. Many young people in areas of the United States isolated from urban airports and other ports of entry are just beginning to meet large groups of people whose first language is not English. Learning enough of a language to be able to speak and read a few phrases helps students to recognize the challenging aspects of another language, and to respect the efforts of people learning English. Finally, knowing a little about another language seems to create a bond with other speakers of that language; recognizing a few words on the radio or television inspires that little "Aha!" of recognition. As irrational as it is, people who know a little about each other's languages are more likely to welcome each other, and that is a step toward global harmony.

CHAPTER 9

Special Populations

ALL EXPERIENCED TEACHERS realize that each student, group, or class is a complicated amalgam of unique traits, so no plan can exactly target all of any specific student's needs. Obviously, this chapter can only make general suggestions for teachers, who will adjust them for each situation.

A. Students whose parents are migrant workers or who work in shifting job markets.

The spotty educational background of these students sometimes makes diagnosis as well as targeted instruction difficult. There is a fear that as soon as the student becomes engaged in classroom activities, his or her tenure will end. Fortunately, a small but increasing number of migrants with children are beginning to settle, as farmers switch to a year-round sequence of crops and industrial work is becoming more available to recent immigrants. The appeal of well-written fiction for young people is that the story motivates language learning more than a textbook, and trade books are designated by grade level; students don't necessarily feel that they are "behind" or working at a lower level.

The use of audio books accompanied by the text is a real hit with many migrant students who can listen and read simultaneously. For three years, one school in North Carolina has signed out tapes and books to their ESL and mostly migrant population on a weekly basis, and, to this date, has lost only one set. Some students report that their parents disapprove of the taped books or treat them as frivolous rewards only to be used after the completion of other homework.

Providing taped books along with the text during silent reading time also helps migrant students "catch up," especially if the book is familiar to other readers in the class. Knowing about the same book as their peers lets new students practice talking about books, increasing their chance to participate equally in the classroom.

Videotapes or abridged versions of longer novels already familiar to other students also provide needed support to English-language learners. Although many teachers avoid "spoiling the ending" or ruining the motivational advantage of suspense for students already competent in English, these aids are valuable as an overview of the book, which allows the new English learner to focus more on details while struggling with new reading vocabulary. The more a student already knows about a story or subject, the more he or she can make the predictions necessary to comprehend the meaning of a passage.

Students who move often need more experiences specific to a school environment. Involve these students in as many opportunities to practice academic verbal and interactive language as possible. Although many migrant students may demonstrate competence in basic interactive communicative skills (BICS), just as many may lack the cognitive academic language proficiency (CALP) that depends on practicing the language of specific content. Stretch the language learning effect of each book by allowing opportunities not only to read a book, but to talk about it, to write about it, and to compare it with other books about similar topics. Let students practice learning in depth rather than trying to introduce them to a wide variety of experiences in order to improve their academic skills.

Welcome these students to your school and classroom by tapping their experiences as resources. As much as possible, ask new students to share their language. While individual greetings and single vocabulary words can raise consciousness of the sounds of different languages, translating phrases and sentences from English to another language can be useful to highlight grammatical constructions indigenous to English for native speakers as well as new learners by comparison or contrast.

Migrant students often have traveled more. Use their experiences in map work, but do not press if students are reluctant to share the whereabouts or travels of their families. Their experiences may have taught them to be wary of revealing too many details of their past.

If possible, encourage your librarian to obtain translations of popular English-language children's books in the language of your students. Their short length and the skillful use of wit and words of good literature make them fun for students to use and share. When new students can act as expert teachers, their self-image often improves, and so does their ability and willingness to act as receptive learners.

Alma Flor Ada's *Gathering the Sun: An Alphabet in Spanish and English*, illustrated by Simon Silva and translated by Rosa Zubizarreta, is a forty-page collection of poetry that would serve as a wonderful welcome while encouraging practice in language skills. The themes of this colorful collection of poems center on the lives of migrant workers in the southwestern United States. Tributes to the vegetables and fruits that gather the colors of the sun into themselves mix with references to Cesar Chavez and the great monuments of Mexico. The rhymes are Spanish, translated into English. This would be suitable for readers at middle school ages and above with a lower intermediate reading proficiency. Encourage all students to practice reading Spanish as well as the English; often even an introduction to another language in print helps native speakers understand grammar and widens vocabulary awareness.

Arthur Dorros's *Radio Man* is a good book to reinforce knowledge of geography while having fun. The main character, Diego from Mexico, listens to the radio, his main friend, as his family travels through the U.S. West, picking fruits and vegetables. The text is in both English and Spanish.

Of course, not all migrant workers are Latino. Sherley Anne Williams's *Working Cotton* is about a young African American girl named Shelan who works cotton near Fresno. The brief text and lovely illustrations, which won a Caldecott Honor in 1993, don't soften the hardships of migrant life, but they do suggest that farming work is not merely bleak. Migrant workers can be resilient and strong-minded, and this book makes that clear.

For older students who can read at the high-intermediate level, Linda Crew's *Children of the River*, mentioned in an earlier chapter, describes the life of Cambodian workers in Oregon. This young adult novel emphasizes one family's struggle between maintaining traditional values and adjusting to American ideas. In high school, Sundara, the main character, befriends a blond, blue-eyed football player, who is attracted by her seriousness and her unique experiences. This rather short novel works well as a read-aloud to motivate discussion among mature students about cross-cultural issues. Another relevant novel is *Esperanza Rising* by Pam Munoz Ryan, published by Scholastic in 2000. It relates the history of Hispanic migrant workers in California just after the Mexican Revolution and the beginnings of unionization.

B. ESL students with physical or mental differences that affect their ability to learn language

Any public school student assessed with physical or mental differences large enough to affect learning is eligible for special services and accommodations to meet the requirements set forth in the 1965 Elementary and Secondary Education Act and the 1968 Bilingual Education Act. Individual education programs (IEPs) should be designed to address learning difficulties that depend on an amalgam of factors: the nature of the disability, the student's level of language proficiency in both his or her native language and in English, and the student's intellectual capacity. Assessing any one of these factors is difficult because the ways most educators measure all three are so intertwined. Students with limited English proficiency have been over-represented in some areas where special services designed for physically or mentally different children are substituted for second-language instruction, or under-represented in such programs when learning difficulties are all blamed on the lack of English proficiency. Accurate assessment and instructional design are understandably difficult. Another factor is that the parental permission necessary for some types of assessment and placement is often more difficult to attain from foreign-born parents than from parents and caretakers familiar with the American system of education.

Accommodations for students with mild learning differences are similar to those for native-language speakers:

Establish a predictable classroom routine that reinforces each student's self-confidence and establishes helpful habits of learning;
Repeat and clarify instructions both aloud and in writing;
Label and demonstrate as well as tell;
Use highly motivating print materials with supporting illustrations, diagrams, and explanations;
Encourage, encourage, encourage.

As much as possible, provide these students with positive learning experiences and opportunities to demonstrate hands-on learning to show that they "get it" and to increase memory retention. If these students can draw, encourage them to illustrate sequences of events of character relationships or meaningful settings ("my home" or "my family") as well as events, characters, and settings from literature. Make cartoons of historical events and flow-charts of causes and effects in history, science, math, grammar, and human relationships. If these students can sing or perform, assign raps, lyrics, and rhythmic drills with math, grammar, chemical elements, dates, and whatever else needs to be memorized. Be generous in your appreciation of their efforts.

Picture books, picture dictionaries, audiotapes, and re-reading help students retain language and material. Fortunately, we have an increasing number of well-written books about students with physical or mental differences who succeed in becoming part of a classroom community. Teachers and other class leaders can model courteous techniques for including students with differences in classroom activities, not as victims who need tolerance but as community members with unusual gifts. Usually, young children are easier to lead; older students may need more motivation. As much as is practical, ask students with both language differences and physical or learning differences to participate in ways that help others. Use them as experts in their native languages or cultures. Ask all members of your classroom community to pool their imagination and intelligence in helping every student, especially those from non-traditional backgrounds, become valuable resources to the class. Do insist on good manners and respect from everyone, including those with visible differences. If students are disruptive, reduce the amount of new stimuli; they may need more predictable consequences for their actions. A helpful resource is the Council for Exceptional Children, Division for Culturally and Linguistically Diverse Exceptional Learners (CLiDES) (1920 Association Drive, Reston, VA 22091; Tel. 703-264-9435).

Because language teaching depends so much on oral communication, students with hearing problems have particular difficulties. Using books written for young people to support more academic texts or lectures is especially helpful. Provide captioned videos and written scripts for students with partial hearing loss, and American Sign Language (ASL) for students with profound hearing loss. A good resource is the Teaching English to Deaf Students (TEDS) Interest Section of TESOL.

C. Students whose cultural backgrounds do not encourage learning styles typical of North American classrooms.

Mainstream Americans share habits of introducing their children to language and literacy that give them an advantage in American classrooms over children who come from cultural backgrounds that perpetuate different habits. For example, most middle-class American caregivers tend to talk with their infants as if they were linguistic equals, asking questions, and repeating responses with more elaborate language. Caregivers in other cultures may tend to relate to their infants in a way that separates adult language from the cooperative communication of their peers. They may use language to correct and to provide information, but not to ask questions or ask for opinions. Literature for children is not as common in many cultures, except among the wealthy. Reading is a skill learned in school and used by adults for business and escape rather than as a pastime practiced between child and parent. In many other cultures, children learn more cooperatively from each other than from individual adults. In American classrooms, cooperation can look like "cheating," and children's language from other cultures can seem more focused on assessing and repeating the opinion of the group rather than expressing individual ideas.

Research and take advantage of your students' cultural capital. Research by asking, What is important to you? What are your goals? Ask the students, their parents, and any other person familiar with the culture. At the same time, try to avoid stereotyping. If your observations of an individual from another culture don't jibe with what you have learned previously, trust your instincts. Everyone has a different story and a different way of telling it. A good resource for information about teaching students from other cultures are the periodic articles featured in *ESL Magazine: The Information Source for ESL/EFL Professionals Worldwide*, online at eslmagazine@compuserve.com.

Include folktales and other traditional literature from your students' cultures among the books you read aloud to younger students or in teaching students to read. These may reflect oral traditions and stories foreign-born students have heard from older relatives and friends. A wide variety of these are published with a fascinating variety of illustrations. Some excellent folktales retold and illustrated as individual books and resources for teaching with them are listed in the bibliography and in the previous two chapters.

Allow students from cooperative cultures to work in partners or small groups. Provide lots of support and practice for students in small groups to talk about picture books, to read aloud, or to discuss ideas from books. When students from other cultures write, look for strengths and charm in the different styles and patterns of logic they may use. English has flowered because its speakers have borrowed freely from other language traditions.

D. Students who are adults

Older students who are beginning to learn any language are particularly vulnerable to feeling inadequate. While children are expected to make mistakes and struggle with language, adults are used to being able to express themselves. Adult students need to be given an extra measure of protection against embarrassment. Unlike other skills, language is so tied to how we present ourselves to others that not being able to speak, read, or write easily seems especially discouraging.

Using children's and young adult literature to teach adults or older teens may seem disrespectful, but if their goal is to learn English, books for children and young adults offer the most natural range of vocabulary and structural practice. Be ready to roll your eyes along with your students if they perceive the material as beneath their dignity. Avoid silly-looking illustrations, a sentimental tone, and personified animals. Fantasy is fine if the illustrations are sophisticated. Fractured fairytales by Jon Sciezka are a good choice for beginning students, for their background knowledge of the traditional tale allows them to focus on the new language; the jokes caused by the twisted endings provide a reward. Various versions of traditional tales from different cultures can also be used. Ed Young's translation of *Lon Po Po: A Red Riding Hood Story from China* with a twenty-seven page simple repetitive text is suitable for beginning adult readers. Engage students in a discussion of the differing values portrayed. In this version, the cleverness of the heroine is admired, rather than her physical beauty or innocence in versions more familiar to most Americans. Another book with a simple brief text but with deep meaning and an appropriate tone for adults is Taro Yashima's *Crow Boy*.

For intermediate-level readers, use appropriate young adult novels to provide practice in fluency. Select short novels with simple plots and settings and a small number of characters to allow readers to become accustomed to the style of a single author and the vocabulary of a story drawn over a longer period of time. Many of Gary Paulsen's adventures motivate readers to read faster, surging ahead to find out what will happen next, but his sensitive treatment of characters also provides meat for discussion. His writing is simple yet lyrical. *Dogsong* packs fourteen chapters in 171 small pages of well-spaced print. After an introductory lesson, many readers are pleased to find that they can read a chapter or even more in a single class session using the routine described in previous chapters. Photos, video clips, and even biographical articles about Paulsen's experiences in the Iditarod will add texture and additional practice in reading this novel. Throughout this book, I have mentioned other texts, including others by Paulsen, suitable in tone and subject matter for adult learners.

Much of the pleasure of teaching English to new learners is finding exactly the right reading matter for each student, books with the right tone, style, illustrations, mood, and shape. Fortunately, we live at a time when choice is in style. Good books can build bridges over the chasm between languages, the visible clues of print and pictures spanning the distance between sound and meaning. Enjoy the journey across.

Bibliography

LITERATURE FOR CHILDREN AND YOUNG ADULTS

Picture Dictionaries

Corbeil, Jean-Claude, and Ariane Archambault. *Scholastic Visual Dictionary.* Scholastic, 2000. (ISBN 0-439-05940-2)

1,000 Palabras en inglés. Berlitz Publishers, 1998. (ISBN 2-8315-6553-7)

Shapiro, Norma, and Jayne Adelson-Goldstein. *The Oxford Picture Dictionary.* Oxford University Press, 1998. (ISBN 0-19-470059-3)

Picture Books

Bang, Molly. *Ten, Nine, Eight.* Greenwillow, 1989. (ISBN 0-688-00906-9)

Bemelmans, Ludwig. *Madeline's Rescue.* Viking Press, 1951. (ISBN 0-670-44716-1)

———. *Rosebud.* Knopf, 1942. (ISBN 0-679-84913-0)

Brown, Margaret Wise. *Goodnight Moon.* Illustrated by Clement Hurd. Harper & Row, 1947. (ISBN 0-064-43017-0)

Brown, Margaret Wise. *The Runaway Bunny.* Illustrated by Clement Hurd. HarperCollins, 1942. (ISBN 0-06-020765-5)

Melmed, Laura Krauss. *I Love You as Much.* Illustrated by Henri Sorenson. Lothrop, Lee & Shepard, 1993. (ISBN 0-688-11718-X)

Morris, Ann. *Bread, Bread, Bread.* Photographs by Ken Hegman. Lothrop, Lee, Shepard, 1989. (ISBN 0-688-06334-9)

Scieszka, Jon. *The True Story of the Three Little Pigs.* Illustrated by Lane Smith. Viking, 1989. (ISBN 0-670-88844-3)

Sendak, Maurice. *Where the Wild Things Are.* HarperCollins, 1963. (ISBN 0-606-03230-4)

————. *In the Night Kitchen.* Harper & Row, 1970. (ISBN 0-06-025489)

Shannon, David. *No, David!* Scholastic, 1998. (ISBN 0-590-93002-8)

Tavares, Matt. *Zachary's Ball.* Candlewick Press, 2000. (ISBN 0-7636-0730-4)

Wiesner, David. *June 29, 1999.* Clarion Books, 1999. (ISBN 0-395-59762-5)

————. *Sector 7.* Clarion Books, 1999. (ISBN 0-395-74656-6)

————. *Tuesday.* Clarion Books, 1991. (ISBN 0-395-55113-7)

RESOURCES FOR TEACHING HISTORY

Adler, David. *Hilde and Eli: Children of the Holocaust.* Illustrated by Karen Ritz. Holiday House, 1995. (ISBN 0-8234-1091-9)

Anderson, Laurie Halse. *Fever 1793.* Simon & Schuster, 2000. (ISBN 0-689-83858-1)

Bailey, Linda, and Bill Slavin. *Adventures in the Middle Ages.* Kids Can Press (Nelvana), 2000. (ISBN 1-55074-540-9)

Borden, Louise. *Sleds on Boston Common: A Story from the American Revolution.* Illustrated by Robert Andrew Parker. Margaret K. McElderry Books, 2000. (ISBN 0-689-82812-8)

Collier, James Lincoln, and Christopher Collier. *The Clock.* Illustrated by Kelly Maddox. Bantam Doubleday, 1992. (ISBN 0-440-40999-3)

————. *My Brother Sam Is Dead.* Four Winds Press, 1975. (ISBN 0-027229807)

Fritz, Jean. *And Then What Happened, Paul Revere?* Illustrated by Margot Tomes. Putnam, 1973. (ISBN 0-399-23337-7)

————. *Can't You Make Them Behave, King George?* Putnam, 1977. (ISBN 0-399-23304-0)

————. *Will You Sign Here, John Hancock?* Illustrated by Trina Shart Hyman. Putnam, 1976. (ISBN 0-69-811440-X)

Fry, Plantagenet Somerset. *The Dorling-Kindersley History of the World.* DK Publishing, 1994. (ISBN 1-56458-244-2)

Greene, Carol. *Thomas Jefferson: Author, Inventor, President.* Children's Press, 1991. (ISBN 0-516-04224-6)

Harness, Cheryl. *Remember the Ladies: 100 Great American Women.* HarperCollins, 2001. ISBN 0-688-17017-X

Hesse, Karen. *Out of the Dust.* Scholastic, 1997. (ISBN 0-590-37125-8)

Hirsch, E. D., Jr. *What Your First Grader Needs to Know*. Delta, 1991, 1997. (ISBN 0-385-31987-8)

Johnston, Johanna. *They Led the Way: 14 American Women*. Illustrated by Deanne Hollinger. Scholastic, 1972. (ISBN 0-590-44431-X)

Lawson, Robert. *Ben and Me: A New and Astonishing Life of Benjamin Franklin as Written by His Good Mouse Amos, Lately Discovered, Edited and Illustrated by Robert Lawson*. Little, Brown, 1939. (ISBN 0-3165-2520-0)

——. *Mr. Revere and I, Being an Account of Certain Episodes in the Career of Paul Revere, Esq. as Recently Revealed by his Horse, Scheherazade, Late Pride of His Royal Majesty's 14th Regiment of Foot, Set Down and Embellished with Numerous Drawings by Robert Lawson*. Little, Brown, 1939, 1988. (ISBN 0-3165-1729-1)

Lowry, Lois. *Number the Stars*. Laurel-Leaf, 1989. (ISBN 0-440-22753-4)

Lyon, George Ella. *Who Came Down that Road?* Illustrated by Peter Catalano. Orchard Books, 1992. (ISBN 0-5310-598-7-1)

Madgwick, Wendy. *Questions and Answers: Ancient Civilizations*. Kingfisher, 2000. (ISBN 0-7534-5310-X)

Millard, Anne. *A Street though Time: A 12,000 Year Walk through History*. Illustrated by Steve Noon. Dorling Kindersley, 1998. (ISBN 0-7894-3426-1)

Millard, Anne, and Patricia Vanags. *The Usborne Book of World History: A Children's Encyclopedia of History*. Usborne, 1985. EDC Publishing, USA (ISBN 0-86020-959-8)

Nelson, Pam (editor). Dawn Chipman, Mari Florence, Naomi Wax. *Cool Women: The Thinking Girl's Guide to the Hippest Women in History*. Girl Press, 1998. (ISBN 0-9659754-0-1)

Paulsen, Gary. *Nightjohn*. Laurel-Leaf Books, 1993. (ISBN 0-440-21936-1)

——. *Sarny*. Laurel-Leaf Books, 1998. (ISBN 0-4402-1973-6)

Roop, Peter, and Connie Roop. *Buttons for General Washington*. Illustrated by Peter E. Hanson. Carolrhoda Books, 1986. (ISBN 0-876142943)

Sewall, Marcia. *The Pilgrims of Plimoth*. Atheneum, 1986, 1996 (ISBN 0-6898-0861-5).

Steele, Philip. *The Medieval World*. Kingfisher, 2000. (ISBN 0-7534-5303-7)

Turner, Ann. *Katie's Trunk*. Macmillan, 1992. (ISBN 0-689-11054-7)

Van Allsburg, Chris Van. *The Z Was Zapped: A Play in Twenty-six Acts*. Houghton Mifflin, 1987. (ISBN 0-395-44612-0)

Wargin, Kathy-jo. *The Legend of Mackinac Island*. Illustrated by Gijsbert van Frankenhuyzen. Sleeping Bear Press, 1999. (ISBN 1-886947-12-0)

Warren, Andrea. *Surviving Hitler: A Boy in the Nazi Death Camps*. Harper, 2001. (ISBN 0-6181-1712-1)

TEACHING MATH AND SCIENCE

AIMS Education Foundation. *Math and Science: A Solution*. 1987 (P.O. Box 8120, Fresno, CA 93747-8120)

Anno, Mitsumasa. *Anno's Math Games*. Penguin Putnam Books, 1997. (ISBN 0-698-11671-2)

——. *Magic Seeds*. Philomel, 1995. (ISBN 0-3992-253-8-2)

Ardley, Neil. *The Science Book of Air*. Harcourt Brace Jovanovich, 1991. (ISBN 0-15-200575-3)

——. *The Science Book of Color*. Harcourt Brace Jovanovich, 1991. (ISBN 0-15-200576-5)

——. *The Science Book of Light*. Harcourt Brace Jovanovich, 1991. (ISBN 0-15-200577-3)

Bang, Molly. *Ten, Nine, Eight*. Greenwillow, 1989. (ISBN 0-688-00906-9)

Bassano, Sharron, and Mary Ann Christison. *Life Sciences: Content and Learning Strategies*. Star Science through Active Reading Series. Addison-Wesley, 1992. (ISBN 0-8013-0347-8)

Burkhardt, Ann. *Apples*. Early Science Readers Series. Bridgestone Books, 1996. (ISBN 1-56065-448-1)

——. *Corn*. Early Science Readers Series. Bridgestone Books, 1996. (ISBN 1-56065-450-3)

——. *Potatoes*. Early Science Readers Series. Bridgestone Books, 1996. (ISBN 1-56065-451-1)

——. *Pumpkins*. Early Science Readers Series. Bridgestone Books, 1996. (ISBN 1-56065-449-X)

Burns, Marilyn. *Math and Literature, K–3, Book One*. Math Solutions, 1992. (ISBN 0-941-35507-1)

Carle, Eric. *The Very Hungry Caterpillar*. Scholastic, 1994. (ISBN 0-399-22269-0-7)

Chinery, Michael. *Seashores*. Illustrated by Wayne Ford. Troll Associates, 1991. (ISBN 84-241-2053-1)

Clemson, David and Wendy Clemson. *My First Math Book.* Dorling Kindersley, 1991. (ISBN 84-272-1926-1)

Cole, Joanna. *The Human Body.* Illustrated by Bruce Deger. Magic School Bus Series. Scholastic, 1989. (ISBN 0-590-41427-5)

Cooper, Jason. *Gardens of the Earth: Trees.* Rourke Enterprises, 1999. (ISBN 0-86592-498-8)

Dahl, Michael. *Inclined Planes.* Early Reader Science Series. Bridgestone Books, 1996. (ISBN 1-56065-444-9)

Demi. *One Grain of Rice: A Mathematical Folktale.* Scholastic, 1997. (ISBN 0-59093998X)

Dudley, Karen. *Bald Eagles.* Untamed World Series. Raintree/Steck-Vaughn, 1998. (ISBN 0-8172-4571-5)

——. *Giant Pandas.* Untamed World Series. Raintree/Steck-Vaughn, 1998. (ISBN 0-8172-4566-9)

——. *Wolves.* Untamed World Series. Raintree/Steck-Vaughn, 1998. (ISBN 0-8172-4561-8)

Duey, Kathleen. American Diaries Series. Aladdin Paperback.

Gardiner, John Reynolds. *Stone Fox.* Harper Trophy, 1980. (ISBN 0-06-440132-4)

George, Jean Craighead. *The Moon of the Deer.* Illustrated by Jean Zallinger. Crowell, 1993. (ISBN 0-0060-20816-3)

——. *My Side of the Mountain.* Dutton, 1959, 1976. (ISBN 0-5253-553-0-8)

——. *There's an Owl in the Shower.* Illustrated by Christine Herman Merrill. HarperCollins, 1995. (ISBN 0-0602-489-1-2)

Glazer, Joan. *Introduction to Children's Literature.* Prentice-Hall, 1997. (ISBN 0-02-344111-9)

Haskins, Jim. *Counting Your Way through Africa.* Carolrhoda, 1989. (ISBN 0-87614-514-4)

Hutchins, Pat. *The Doorbell Rang.* Greenwillow, 1986. (ISBN 0-6880-923-4-9)

Juster, Norton. *The Dot and the Line: A Romance in Lower Mathematics.* SeaStar, 1963, 2001. (ISBN 1-58717-069-8)

King, Andrew. *Math for Fun Projects.* Copper Beech, 1999. (ISBN 0-7613-0789-3)

Levine, Marie. *Great White Sharks.* Untamed World Series. Raintree/Steck-Vaughn, 1998. (ISBN 0-8172-4569-3)

Meyer, Carolyn. *Anastasia: The Last Grand Duchess.* Royal Diaries. Scholastic, 2000. (ISBN 0-439129087)

Scieszka, Jon. *Math Curse.* Illustrated by Lane Smith.Viking, 1995. (ISBN 0-670-86194-4)

Selsam, Margaret. *The Amazing Dandelion.* Photographs by Jerome Wexler. William Morrow, 1977. (ISBN 0-688-22129-7)

Spense, Margaret. *Fossil Fuel.* Gloucester Press, 1993. (ISBN 0-531-17394-1)

Wick, Walter. *A Drop of Water: A Book of Science and Wonder.* Scholastic Press, 1997. (ISBN 0-590-22197)

————. *Optical Tricks.* Scholastic, 1998. (ISBN 0-590-11711-4)

MULTICULTURAL THEMES

Bridges, Ruby. *Through My Eyes.* Edited by Margo Lundell. Scholastic, 1999. (ISBN 0-590-18923-9)

Clare, John. *North American Indian Life.* Barrons Educational Series, 2000. (ISBN 0-7641-1071-3)

Coles, Robert. *The Story of Ruby Bridges.* Illustrated by George Ford. Scholastic, 1995. (ISBN 0-590-43967-7)

Crew, Donald. *Big Mama.* Greenwillow Books, 1991. (ISBN 0-688-09950-5)

Crew, Linda. *Children of the River.* Delacorte, 1989. (ISBN 0-440-2102-2-4)

Friedman, R. *How My Parents Learned to Eat.* Illustrated by Allen Say. Houghton Mifflin, 1984. (ISBN 0-395-3537-9-3)

Johnston, Tony. *The Iguana Brothers: Presenting a Tale of Two Lizards.* Illustrated by Mark Teague. Blue Sky Press, 1995. (ISBN 0-590-47468-5)

Kamma, Anne. *If You Lived with the Hopi.* Illustrated by Linda Gardner. Scholastic, 1999. (ISBN 0-590-45162-6)

Keats, Ezra Jack. *The Snowy Day.* Putnam, 1962, 1996. (ISBN 0-670-86733-0)

Mazer, Ann, ed. *America Street: A Multicultural Anthology of Stories.* Persea Books, 1993. (ISBN 0-89255-191-7)

McGovern, Ann. *If You Lived with the Sioux.* Illustrated by Jean Syverud Drew. Scholastic, 1974, 1992. (ISBN 0-590-45162-6)

Mochizuki, Ken. *Baseball Saved Us.* Illustrated by Dom Lee. Lee and Low Books, 1993. (ISBN 1-88000-019-9)

Myers, Walter Dean. *Now Is Your Time: The African-American Struggle for Freedom.* Harper, 1991. (ISBN 0-064-4612-0-3)

——. *Harlem: A Poem.* Illustrated by Christopher Myers. Scholastic, 1997. (ISBN 0-590-5434-0-7)

Namoika, Lensey. *Yang the Second and Her Secret Admirers.* Dell Yearling, 1998. (ISBN 0-440-41641-8)

——. *Yang the Third and Her Impossible Family.* Dell Yearling, 1995. (ISBN 0-440-41231-5)

——. *Yang the Youngest and His Terrible Ear.* Dell Yearling, 1992. (ISBN 0-440-40917-9)

Osinski, Alice. *The Navajo.* Children's Press, 1987, 1992. (ISBN 0-516-01236-3)

Rosa-Casanova, Sylvia. *Mama Provi and the Pot of Rice.* Illustrated by Robert Roth. Atheneum, 1997. (ISBN 0-689-31932-0)

Say, Allen. *Grandfather's Journey.* Houghton Mifflin, 1993. (ISBN 0-395-5703-5-2)

——. *Tree of Cranes.* Houghton Mifflin, 1991. (ISBN 0-395-52024-X)

Schuch, Steve. *A Symphony of Whales.* Illustrated by Peter Sylvada. Harcourt Brace & Company, 1999. (ISBN 0-151-00289-4)

Soto, Gary. *Baseball in April and Other Stories.* Harcourt Brace Jovanovich, 1990. (ISBN 0-15-205721-8)

——. *Buried Onions.* Harcourt Brace and Company, 1997. (ISBN 0-15-201333-4)

——. *Snapshots from the Wedding.* Illustrated by Stephanie Garcia. G. P. Putnam's, 1997. (ISBN 0-39922808X)

Tallchief, Maria, with Rosemary Wells. *Tallchief: America's Prima Ballerina.* Illustrated by Gary Kelley. Viking, 1999. (ISBN 0-670-88756-0)

Walker, Alice. *To Hell with Dying.* Illustrated by Catherine Deeter. Harcourt Brace Jovanovich, 1967, 1988. (ISBN 0-15-28907-5)

Wingate, Philippa, and Steven Reid. *Who Were the First North Americans?* Illustrated by David Cuzik. Usborne Publishers, 1998. (ISBN 0-7460-2040-6)

WHEN MOST STUDENTS DON'T SPEAK ENGLISH

Aardema, Verna. *Borreguita and the Coyote.* Illustrated by Petra Mathers. Knopf, 1991. (ISBN 0-679-80921-X)

Dorros, Arthur. *Abuela.* Illustrated by Elisa Kleven. Dutton, 1991. (ISBN 0-525-4475-0-4)

———. *Por fin es carnaval. (Tonight Is Carnaval)*. Photographs by Club de Madres Virgen. Translated by Sandra Marulanda Dorros. Puffin/Warne Penguin, 1995. (ISBN 0-14-055471-8)

Feder, Jane. *Table, Chair, Bear: A Book in Many Languages*. Houghton-Mifflin, 1997. (ISBN 0-3958-5075-4)

Mora, Pat. *Listen to the Desert/Oye al desierto*. Illustrated by Francisco Mora. Houghton Mifflin, 1994. (ISBN 0-395-67292-9)

Paulsen, Gary. *Sisters/Hermanas*. Translated by Gloria de Aragon Andujar. Harcourt Brace, 1993. (ISBN 0-590-48141-X)

Winter, Jonah. *Diego*. Illustrated by Jeanette Winter. Translated by Amy Prince. Knopf, 1991 (ISBN 0-679-81987-8)

SPECIAL POPULATIONS

Ada, Alma Flor. *Gathering the Sun: An Alphabet in Spanish and English*. Illustrated by Simon Silva. Translated by Rosa Zubizarreta. Lothrop, Lee & Shepard, 1997. (ISBN 0-688-13903-5)

Crew, Linda. *Children of the River*. Delacorte, 1989. (ISBN 0-440-2102-2-4)

Dorros, Arthur. *Radio Man/Don Radio*. Translated by Sandra M. Dorros. Bradbury Books, 1990. (ISBN 0-027-7078-0-8)

Paulsen, Gary. *Dogsong*. Bradbury Press, 1985. (ISBN 0-027-7018-0-8)

Ryan, Pam Munoz. *Esperanza Rising*. Scholastic, 2000. (ISBN 0-439-1204-1)

Williams, Sherley Anne. *Working Cotton*. Illustrated by Carole Byard. Harcourt, 1992. (ISBN 0-1-529-9624-9)

Yashima, Taro. *Crow Boy*. Puffin, 1955. (ISBN 0-14-05017-2-X)

Young, Ed. *Lon Po Po: A Red Riding Hood Story from China*. Philomel/Penguin, 1989. (ISBN 0-698-11382-9)

Selected Annotated Bibliography
of Resources for Teachers

Clarke, Mark, Barbara Dobson, and Sandra Silberstein. *Choice Readings*. University of Michigan Press, 1996. (ISBN 0-472-08329-5) Eight chapters, 260 pages. Each chapter deals with a different reading skill, for intermediate students. Begins with airline terminal maps, how to break down difficult sentences by crossing out (mentally or physically) unfamiliar vocabulary. Questions, exercises, and strategies to focus attention on important facts. Good sections on non-prose reading (charts, timetables, dictionaries, maps, a college application, letters, campus map, newspaper article).

Collie, Joanne, and Stephen Slater. *Literature Language Classroom: A Resource Book of Ideas and Activities*. Cambridge University Press, 1997. (ISBN 0-521-31224-8) A collection of learning activities with thorough explanations and theoretical rationales. Especially helpful for secondary school classrooms.

Dunn, Opal. *Help Your Child with a Foreign Language*. Berlitz, 1994. (ISBN 2-8315-6806-4) Written for parents, this easy-to-read paperback summarizes issues about second-language learning and offers numerous ideas and tips for learning at the basic level. This would be useful for tutors. An appendix lists about seventy-five phrases in French, Spanish, German, and Italian.

Echevarria, Jane, and Anne Graves. *Sheltered Content Instruction: Teaching English-Language Learners with Diverse Abilities*. Allyn & Bacon, 1998. (ISBN 0-205-16874-4) This scholarly textbook is dense with helpful background information, ideas, and examples of ways to modify presentation and resources of content material for ESL students.

ESL Magazine: The Information Source for ESL/EFL Professionals Worldwide, Bridge Press (ISSN 1098-6553), online at eslmagazine@ compuserve.com. A reasonably priced bimonthly magazine with readable articles about teaching English in educational and business institutions all over the globe. This is a worthwhile resource for all language educators.

Faltis, Christian J., and Sarah J. Hudelson. *Bilingual Education in Elementary and Secondary School Communities: Toward Understanding and Caring*. Allyn & Bacon, 1998. (ISBN 0-205-17120-6) A comprehensive description, history, and theoretical rationale for bilingual education, this academic text contains many useful examples.

Faltis, Christian J. *Joinfostering: Teaching and Learning in Multicultural Classrooms*. Prentice-Hall, 2001. (ISBN 0-13-017913-2) An overview of the theories, history, and strategies for teaching in a multilingual setting, this textbook for prospective teachers is a good resource.

Farber, Barry. *How to Learn Any Language: Quickly, Easily, Inexpensively, Enjoyably, and On Your Own*. Citadel, 1991, 1993. (ISBN 0-8065-1271-7) A good motivational conversation about the advantages, joys, and quick methods for learning a second language, this would be fun to include in a classroom library for middle school and above students. The author expresses his opinions about the comparative difficulty of languages, and presents many interesting facts and ideas. This may raise the status of new learners of English to valuable resources for budding linguists and travelers.

Freeman, Yvonne S., and David E. Freeman. *ESL/EFL Teaching: Principles for Success*. Heinemann, 1998. (ISBN 0-325-00079-4) This text for teachers by experienced bilingual teachers and trainers of English teachers lays out clear arguments for whole language methods of teaching new learners of English and ends with strong support and specific recommendations for bilingual education.

Fuller, Graham. *How to Learn a Foreign Language*. Storm King Press, 1987. (ISBN 0-935166-02-5) A breezy, fast-paced brief conversation about the language families, sounds, and formats that might be attractive to middle school and high school learners interested in learning basic linguistic relationships.

Gibbons, Pauline. *Learning to Learn a Second Language*. Primary English Teaching Association, Heinemann, 1991. (ISBN 0-435-08785-1) This clear, concise introduction to principles and methods of teaching ESL is based on many years of teaching in many situations. The 119 pages include straightforward advice, explanations, and directions for useful strategies.

Hakuta, Kenji. *Mirror of Language: The Debate on Bilingualism*. Basic Books, 1986. (ISBN 0-465-04637-1) A brief historical overview of the issues surrounding the practice of using students' dominant language for part of their instruction while they are learning English.

Harvey, William M. S. *Inglés para Latinos*. Barrons Educational Series, 1992. (ISBN 0-8120-4781-8) English from a Latino point of view, explained in Spanish, with motivating tips about language learning in Spanish. Ten chapters—beginning with the recognition of cognates in English, first words, the alphabet, numbers, time, calendar, weather, people—progress to short conversational chapters. This looks like a great motivator for people literate in Spanish, a good start for children, and a useful bridge for bilingual education.

Krashen, Stephen. *Principles and Practice in Second Language Acquisition*. New York: Pergamon Press, 1982.

Kress, Jacqueline E. *The ESL Teacher's Book of Lists*. The Center for Applied Research in Education, 1993. (ISBN 0-87628-307-5) This handy compendium of common vocabulary, expressions, cognates, academic vocabularies, grammatical rules and exceptions, pronunciation hints, assessment measures, and resources for any aspect of ESL teaching you can imagine is useful, easy-to-use, and kind of fun! It includes games, themes, ideas, and even a glossary of ESL jargon.

McCaffery, Laura Hibbets. *Building an ESL Collection for Young Adults: A Bibliography of Recommended Fiction and Nonfiction for Schools and Public Libraries*. Greenwood Press, 1998. (ISBN 0-313-29937-4) Organized by Library of Congress subject headings, this annotated bibliography was selected by the author for use by young people and adults in public education and libraries. These books were selected because their format and illustrations are attractive and appropriate, their content is interesting and relevant to most curriculum subjects, and they are written in a concise and clear style. The reading level is indicated, as measured by the Fry Reading Scale, and varies between grades three and eight. Subjects include adventure and mystery, biographies, life skills, ethnic diversity, sports, nature, and science. Selections include both trade books and books published as ESL materials, fiction and nonfiction. The appendices include lists of both print and nonprint materials, along with contact information. This volume would be useful for librarians and teachers building a collection for low intermediate levels.

Norton, Donna. *Multicultural Children's Literature: Through the Eyes of Many Children.* Merrill Prentice Hall, 2001. (ISBN 0-13-243122-X) A textbook analysis of African American, Native American, Latino, Asian, Jewish, and Middle Eastern multicultural literature for children. Each section is introduced by a time line, and contains a discussion of traditional and folk lore, historical fiction and nonfiction, contemporary realistic fiction and nonfiction, and teaching strategies. This volume is very complete and scholarly, but not difficult to read and use.

Pratt, Linda, and Janice J. Beaty. *Transcultural Children's Literature.* Prentice Hall, 1999. (ISBN 0-13-432816-7) This excellent resource on children's books about other cultures for teachers has an extensively annotated bibliography of children's texts, mostly picture books, divided geographically by the nations they portray, and also includes classroom applications.

Rubin, Joan, and Irene Thompson. *How to Be a More Successful Language Learner.* Heinle and Heinle, 1994. (ISBN 0-8384-4734-1) A handy, easy-to-read, brief, and upbeat book about how to learn, this is a good reminder for teachers of what they have absorbed previously about language learning. Tutors and volunteers will recognize a lot of good common sense.

Schinke-Llano, Linda, and Rebecca Rauff, editors. *New Ways in Teaching Young Children.* New Ways in TESOL Series II. Series Editor, Jack C. Richards. TESOL, 1996. (ISBN 0-9397-9-1633) This is a collection of over eighty teaching exercises organized by overall methods (the senses, learning through actions, drama, storytelling, music), each a page long with instructions, materials, advice, and caveats. Although aimed at teachers of young children, some of the ideas could be adjusted for any age of beginning language students. Easy-to-use and direct.

Schon, Isabel. *Recommended Books in Spanish for Children and Young Adults, 1996 through 1999.* Scarecrow Press, 2000. (ISBN 0-8108-3840-0) This annotated bibliography of over a thousand books in print includes critical commentaries that are long and descriptive enough to be helpful, outlining the contents and identifying useful information such as reading level, number of pages, and language style and tone.

Shulman, Myra. *Journeys through Literature.* University of Michigan Press, 1995. (ISBN 0-472-08296-5) This advanced-level workbook for selected British and American works of literature includes preview and review questions, a glossary of literary terms, and introductory notes. Appendices include worksheets on writing literary analysis, essays, and poetry.

Small, R. "Teaching the Junior Novel." *English Journal* 61 (2), (1972): 222–229.

Tomlinson, Carl M. *Children's Books from Other Countries.* Scarecrow Press, 1998. (ISBN 0-8108-3447-2) After an introductory section defining international children's literature and tracing its history, especially in the United States, this annotated bibliography of over 700 volumes includes a section on activities for sharing these books with children.

Index